NAVIGATING
DIVORCE
—— *with a* ——
PEACEFUL HEART

A PRACTICAL GUIDE TO CULTIVATING
INNER PEACE IN THE MIDST OF CHAOS

STEPHANIE MERIAUX, CPCC, ACC

Publishing Services provided by Paper Raven Books

Cover design by Rafael Mattey
https://www.instagram.com/rafaelmattey

Author headshot by Chinatsu Earney
https://www.facebook.com/athousandsummersphotography

Printed in the United States of America

First Printing, 2020

Paperback ISBN= 978-1-7354626-0-8
Hardback ISBN= 978-1-7354626-1-5

DEDICATION

Thank you to my steadfast crew—my ballast, my wholehearted supporters:

My parents, Nancy and Gary, who are unwavering in their commitment and dedication to family, growth, and conscious living. You are such an immense support and blessing in my life, and I am grateful for you every day. Mom, thank you for diving in deep with me and accompanying me through the details. When there are critical, time-consuming tasks I need help with, you genuinely set aside everything else to earnestly journey with me. Dad, thank you for maintaining my foundation so that I may have ease and reliability in my daily life.

My evolutionary ally and partner Brad, who came into my life six weeks after my separation. You have witnessed all the undulations and nuances of my inner journey post-separation and have shown me what it means to be deeply, unconditionally loved by a partner. What a gift it was when you shared with me your first impression of my book: that it so authentically represents who I am, what I believe, and how I navigated my divorce. That couldn't have been a better compliment. Thank you for seeing me so fully.

My dear friend Rob, who knew my heart deeply during the most raw period of my life. You saw—and helped me reconnect to—the beauty within me. You replenished my spirit with your presence, wisdom, integrity, and wrap-around bear hugs. With you and the Chipmunks by my side, I began my healing.

My beautiful grandmother Sue, who always encouraged me to write and publish. You were the third person to ever read this manuscript. I gave it to you Wednesday and you finished it in less than 24 hours. The next morning, you fell, broke your hip, and journeyed on to Heaven two weeks later; I made the final edits to this book as I held vigil at your bedside. You are an inspiration—a model of grace, courage, elegance, faith, generosity of spirit, and genuine love. If I embody even half of the qualities you so innately live by, mine will be a life well-lived.

My siblings and their spouses, who remain strong and supportive, showing unconditional love for one another as we navigate through this messy human experience.

And finally, my blessed children. I'm so sorry that you have to grow up in a divorced family. I ache that you ache. I hope we have made your way as healing as possible, given the circumstances. You are my light, my dream come true, and the fulfillment of the biggest desire of my life. Thank you, precious kidlets, for the privilege of being your mommy. I am here for you, with you; always yours.

NAVIGATING
DIVORCE
with a
PEACEFUL HEART

TABLE OF CONTENTS

INTRODUCTION

You do not marry expecting to divorce, yet here you are.

Divorce is an arduous process and every journey is different: different circumstances, different histories, different considerations, different outcomes, different lives, and different hearts.

Regardless of the circumstances or the extremity of our respective situations, if you are divorcing, you and I share the commonality of being thrown from our status quo into the emotional, financial, physical, and spiritual tempest that is divorce.

Be tender with yourself; be compassionate. Grieve for the dream that once was. Embrace the shifts and changes gently. Allow yourself the time and spaciousness to rebuild your identity and your sense of self. You will emerge; you will have grown; you will be wiser.

I feel blessed that my journey includes close, wholehearted supporters and that my ex-husband is a man who, at his core, is a good person and a good father. This has alleviated so much suffering from my own journey—and I know others are not as lucky.

As I share parts of my journey, I do not, in any way, mean to imply blame, judgment, or negative perspectives about my former spouse; neither am I implying that either of us was able to navigate divorce any better than the other, or that either of us contributed more or less toward peace and healing. We have each had our own experience, and I believe we have respectively been doing our best as we navigate through this process. Even still, our journey has included intense hurt, heartbreak, anger, tension, and upheaval, as any divorce would.

Regardless of the details of your situation, if you are divorcing, you could probably use some healing, clarity, tenderness, compassion, and stability. It is my hope that by sharing the principles in this book, it will ease some of your suffering, help you find your footing, and guide you toward more inner peace, strength, and grounding.

As you read, please adapt the language to your situation. Perhaps you're in a same-gender relationship, not a heterosexual one; perhaps you were in a long-term relationship, not a marriage; perhaps you're still married, but considering divorce. The principles still apply, so please adjust accordingly. Similarly, I use the terms "partner" and "former partner" somewhat interchangeably; please adapt as needed, depending on where you are in your journey of marriage, separation, or divorce. When I write as if in the context of marriage, it is not because I assume you are still married. Rather, it is to aid in healing by bringing awareness to what might have been present *during* the marriage.

If even one of these principles touches you, offers you hope, or gives you insight that informs your journey in a positive way, please share this resource with others.

If you are a parent or loved one of someone going through divorce and you are longing to be of service to them during their time of need, please share this resource with them.

You could be the transformational key in someone's journey, simply by sharing this book with them. You never know what tidbit is going to unlock the chains that have kept someone shackled. Sometimes all it takes is one meaningful metaphor, one new perspective, or one shared experience to liberate them and open the way for growth and healing. This book could be that key. YOU could be that key. The world needs more hope and healing, more positive perspectives, more richness, wisdom, and grace. You could be an instrumental part of that, just by sharing this resource with them.

If you are going through divorce or are struggling to recover from one, it is my hope and deep wish that you will continue to evolve, navigating through this journey with an increasingly peaceful heart and sense of inner grounding. Some days will look better than others. Keep your eyes on the goal and your focus fixed—even if you take two steps forward and one step back, you are moving in the right direction!

May you be well, may you be loved,
and may your heart be at peace.

NAVIGATING DIVORCE
WITH A PEACEFUL HEART

Divorce.

Such a seismic shift on life's path; a shattered vision of what life was supposed to be. Dreams dissolve. Life is turned up on end. The person you thought you would never be, you now are. Children's hearts are torn. The shadow sides deep within us, that we've never known, emerge.

The person we once held so dear, the person who inspired tears of joy on our wedding day, is someone we might now be approaching with distrust, bitterness, and resentment.

Paths may diverge completely, or lives may remain intricately tied together due to children or other shared connections. Regardless, a former spouse makes an imprint on one's soul. They continue to show up, perhaps only as memories recalled or stories told, but a part of who you are nonetheless. They invoke feelings in you that continue to color who you are and who you are becoming.

It is thus imperative that you not let the anger of divorce fester and become painful scar tissue. "But how?" you may ask. "How can I start down this journey of healing when my wounds are so raw and my anger so intense?"

You must continually massage your tender heart—acknowledging the hurt and pain, while aspiring to look upon your former spouse with *true kindness, empathy, and generosity of spirit.*

If you're thinking this is unattainable, only possible if the other person drastically changes their ways, or available to you only in the distant future, you are not alone. We tend to live in a world of duality—a black-and-white world of "either/or." It's either one thing or the other. Many of us think *I'm in so much pain! I can't possibly look with kindness on the source of that pain right now!*

Yet, for the sake of your healing, I want to offer you a perspective shift: Embrace this as a non-duality. Tell yourself instead: *I am experiencing a lot of pain AND I can look upon my former partner with kindness.* This gentleness of heart can start now, *before* your own pain has subsided. Acknowledging that *both things are simultaneously possible* can open the door for healing and promote rebirth. It allows you to find yourself again and to navigate through the turmoil while maintaining a peaceful heart.

I did. Here's how…

SECTION 1

CHALLENGE YOUR
EXISTING PARADIGM

More often than not, we associate divorce with inevitable feelings of pain, anger, contentiousness, mistrust, and bitterness. Entertaining the idea that you could go through divorce with a peaceful heart may seem incomprehensible and improbable, especially when you're in the thick of it.

If you are in the midst of divorce or have recently come out of one, you may be overwhelmed with a plethora of negative feelings. This is totally normal and understandable. You are probably operating under an existing framework of beliefs, behaviors, and thought processes that are, by default, impeding your healing and not serving you well.

The good news is, you can start to shift this framework and in so doing, cultivate a more peaceful heart.

Let me be clear: This process will not *eliminate* those negative feelings and experiences. It is not an all-or-nothing endeavor; you will not magically shift from feeling debilitated by pain to being free of pain. You will, however, notice that feelings of intrinsic peace, strength, and clarity gradually begin to supersede the pain and anger.

"Peace. It does not mean to be in a place with no noise, trouble, or hard work. It is to be in the midst of these things and still be calm in your heart."
—Author unknown

The more you focus on shifting your mental framework and integrating these concepts into your heart and mind, the more at peace you will feel. It is a gradual process, yet any strides you make toward enhancing your inner peace through this tumultuous time are more than worth it and will transform your experience of divorce.

A New Paradigm Calls for New Rules

As Albert Einstein said:

> *"The definition of insanity is doing the same thing over and over again, but expecting different results."*

We all operate from an individual subconscious framework that governs how we think, feel, and behave. This framework is made up of rules, values, expectations, beliefs, assumptions, and wisdom that are acquired through our upbringing, our society, our religion, and our life experiences. We are so used to operating under this acquired framework that most of us don't even realize it's there, nor do we recognize the implicit rules that govern it.

During divorce, this paradigm may subtly constrict our experience, perpetuating anger and bitterness of heart. It often seems as though we have no choice in the matter: Regardless of whether or not we wanted to separate from our spouse, we find ourselves in the midst of a contentious, tumultuous divorce and we become victims of circumstance and of our partner's choices and behavior. We assume these negative feelings are part of the process and accept them as par for the course. However, this is a false assumption.

We are, in fact, *at choice* about how we respond to our challenges in life.

If you want to disempower the negative feelings and open up the space for a more peaceful heart to emerge, you will need to shift some of the subconscious beliefs, assumptions, and structures that are keeping your heart constricted. By challenging the rigidity of some of these foundational ways of thinking, you can start that shift, if ever so subtly, and open the door for new perspectives, responses, and emotions to arise.

The first section of this book identifies some of the most common beliefs in this framework and challenges you to subtly shift the beliefs that are limiting your healing and keeping you stuck in a holding pattern of fear, anger, hurt, resentfulness, bitterness, and revenge. At first, challenging these beliefs may feel almost repulsive to you, especially if you've had a traumatic divorce, are deeply entrenched in your bitterness and rage, or have firmly held values. That's fine—notice that reaction and keep reading.

The goal is not to completely overturn your framework of beliefs. It is simply to challenge the black-and-white nature of the framework you've probably been operating under for most of your life without having given much thought to it. Even by *considering* the possibility that these assumptions and beliefs are perhaps not as bulletproof or watertight as you once thought, you are starting to ease the rigid confines of your heart and mind that have ultimately been holding you prisoner to those negative feelings.

Let yourself experience this book with an open heart and an open mind. Let the concepts land softly, gently permeating the well house of your thinking. When you feel resistance, it may be because you are being asked to step outside your comfort zone and challenged to grow. When this happens, take a moment: pause and breathe, consciously relaxing your body and soul.

The very act of reading this book will trigger the process of broadening your perspective and softening your heart so that you can start to embrace a shifted framework. You are being offered a new way of operating: one that supports healing, evolution, and inner peace.

To begin, let's look at the neuroscience behind this tendency to develop rigid, well-defined, all-or-nothing, black-and-white mental frameworks.

Your Brain Wants to Categorize

Duality is a simple framework for our brains to understand: something either is, or isn't; either he is mean, or he isn't; either she is trustworthy, or she isn't; either he's a good dad, or he's not; either I'm at fault, or I'm not. When we categorize using this simple, dualistic mode of thinking, it's easy for our brains to grasp the nature of the thing, thus making our assessment and decision-making process more straightforward. It's easier to feel good about our choices because "we understand the situation so well."

In other words, categorization is our brain's way of organizing and labeling the world around us so that it's easier to understand and respond to. The study of this simplicity theory is found in fields such as philosophy, cognitive science, mathematics, neuro-science, and artificial intelligence. It essentially comes down to the basic human tendency that "the mind seeks the simplest available interpretation of observations"—even if that means giving up a more robust model that is more difficult to understand yet more accurately reflects reality.[1] Basically, when we interpret the world around us, we subconsciously simplify in order to understand, even though in doing so we sacrifice fullness and accuracy.

In reality, life is not black-and-white; there are always variant shades of gray. Your husband may have made some poor choices as a father and at the same time can still be a good dad. Your wife can be an overall trustworthy person yet have also done things that have broken your trust. Someone can be a health fanatic and eat an occasional ice-cream bar or bag of chips. It does not have to be "either/or." In fact, it is most often some of both.

The more you can broaden your perspective and understanding of your partner and allow that both things can be true even though they seem at odds, the more you will be able to tune into a more comprehensive, well-rounded picture of the actuality before you. In so doing, you are consciously combatting the instinct to simplify and are, instead, attempting to see things as they really are.

Is it possible for your husband to be loyal to your family, even though he committed adultery? You might be inclined to answer with a black-and-white "no" response, though I challenge you to invite exploration of the shades of gray:

- To which parts of your family is he loyal?
- In which ways is he even *fiercely* loyal to your family?
- In which ways is he disloyal?

I assure you, both are present and both are true: He is disloyal in some ways and loyal in others. When you focus only on one part of the equation (which most often ends up being the negative part), you lose sight of all the ways in which the other part of the equation is, in fact, true as well.

In the case of the adulterous husband, it is easy to assert, "My husband committed adultery. Therefore, he doesn't love me, doesn't care about his family, is not committed to us, and doesn't care about keeping our family together." In actuality, it is fully possible that he *deeply loves* his family, *is devastated* thinking about his family potentially breaking up, and *longs achingly* to reconnect with his wife but doesn't know how to get there. And that—while truly and deeply feeling this way—he chose to fall into the arms of another woman who was open and eager to show him love (albeit in an unhealthy way). She filled his ache and need for love and connection. Both were true for him—the good and the bad. He deeply loved his family, yet he also loved the way he felt with the other woman.

From the perspective of the wife under the old framework of thinking, it is an "either/or": "Either he loves me or he doesn't," "Either he's faithful and committed to our family or he's not." It leaves no room for error; no room for being a well-intentioned yet messy human (which all of us are, in some way or another).

Just as you wouldn't disregard the affair by thinking, "He loves me, so the affair was meaningless to him," it is just as detrimental to disregard his love for you by thinking, "He had an affair, so our love is meaningless to him."

One does not beget the other. It is not usually an all-or-nothing, black-and-white, "either/or" situation. Again, the truth is that both are probably true, in varying shades of gray.

As humans, we tend to have difficulty sincerely opening our minds to *allow* for both to be true. It is complicated for our minds to comprehend that they both can be true because it goes against our natural tendency to want to classify, label, sort through, and organize everything into neat and tidy, easy-to-understand boxes. When it's one or the other, it's easier to know what to do about it. When we are confronted with shades of gray and the possibility that two conflicting states of heart might be simultaneously true, the mind becomes befuddled in the face of paradox and our path forward becomes much less clear.

In these cases, allow yourself the space to not make a decision yet. The easy way out is to judge and classify. The harder way out is to sit in the complexity and sift through the many parts at play.

By broadening your perspective and allowing space to explore all of the truths that are present, you allow yourself the gift of a more multifaceted view of what is going on; you get a more complete picture of the situation before you. Again, this is challenging to do when you're first shifting your framework. Everything within you might scream to make judgments and decide for yourself what is true. We have an innate need to classify, understand, and wrap everything up with a tidy bow.

When you find yourself making definitive statements such as "my wife is a liar," it is an indication that this is an opportunity to pause and broaden your perspective and understanding. Yes, your wife may have lied and may have even lied many times. And, it is also true that your wife has *not* lied many times. It is therefore true that she is also a truth teller. Look for evidence to support both sides and get curious about it—you will paint a more complete picture of the reality before you. Leaning away from judgment and into curiosity is the first step in shifting your framework.

Replace judgment with curiosity.

This mantra alone can have the power to change how you live your life. It helps orient you away from judgment (which creates divisiveness) and into connection. Even if you don't understand or agree with the person in front of you, replacing judgment with curiosity shows you are interested in them and are open to hearing more about what they are experiencing. You want to see them more deeply, and this is a gift.

People Can Behave Uncharacteristically in Times of Extreme Stress

When you are distressed, you may make choices that are out of character. They may even be totally contrary to your deeply held beliefs and values. Consider the following:

Let's say you (like most of us) believe that stealing is wrong. It is morally something you shouldn't do. Through most of life, it is easy to live in accordance with this value. You stand by this belief, have no reason to question it, and may find it easy to judge people who steal as being immoral or lacking in character or values.

Consider a scenario in which your life suddenly changes. Your family is no longer in stasis and you find yourself in extreme financial scarcity. You no longer have money or government assistance to buy food. Your children begin to ache with hunger. You see their precious little selves withering away—they begin losing weight, energy, and the life in their eyes. You feel helpless and desperate. One day, you stumble across an opportunity to steal food—a simple loaf of bread or a few apples from a fruit stand. You might, in a moment of desperation, decide to steal.

It is not something you would do under normal circumstances. You don't agree with it; you don't condone it; you're not proud of doing it; you hope you never feel compelled to do it again. And yet, it has filled an urgent need—a hole in your life that felt raw, aching, and dire.

This choice of yours does not mean that your character, morals, or values have necessarily changed. It means you have made a choice in a given moment and under a particular set of circumstances. Absolutely, it was your choice and you should be held accountable. Yet, knowing the circumstances, it becomes a little more understandable why you may have made it.

If one steps out of judgment and into curiosity, they will perhaps soften their view of you, knowing that this was a choice made in extreme circumstances; it was made out of desperation and may not be an accurate reflection of your fundamental values. A person can wholeheartedly believe that stealing is wrong yet be driven to steal if their situation is dire enough.

Instead of judging one's character,
consider their circumstances.

This scenario of stealing when faced with starvation is one that is perhaps relatively easy to wrap our heads around because many aspects of it are visible, concrete, and easy to label. There is no money for food, your children are losing muscle mass and energy, there is actual food within swiping range, and you know that feeding this food to your children will provide nourishment, hope, and sustenance for them. There is a logical sequence of cause and effect; it is easy to identify the factors at play and the decisions are tangible and obvious. Either you have money in your pocket or you don't; either you take the food or you don't.

Given the extenuating circumstances, which are relatively easy to identify here, we may find ourselves inclined to offer grace.

Extreme Stress Can Also Be More Subtle

When the factors at play are more obscure, immeasurable, or harder to identify, it becomes less of a black-and-white, easy-to-understand scenario.

For example, consider a wife who is feeling deprived of love and support—she feels ignored and emotionally neglected by her husband, and sees little signs of that changing, despite her best efforts to engage with him.

One day, she eats lunch with a colleague and really enjoys herself. How fabulous to feel a connection with someone again! How nourishing it feels to actually be appreciated by someone! Lunch was harmless—just colleagues hanging out. They begin to eat with each other more often—it feels so refreshing. Soon, the feeling of being seen, supported, and appreciated becomes intoxicating and almost addictive. One day, they exchange their habitual hug after lunch and it escalates into a kiss. They suddenly find themselves in the throes of a budding affair.

The seeds were planted, took root, and sprouted beneath the topsoil without any visible, explicit signs or missteps. Perhaps they knew the soil was ripe for such a connection, but their interactions seemed innocuous enough. Given each person's strong values, an affair seemed unlikely. After all, there wasn't anything blatantly wrong until the hug spun out of control. But now, the seed had blossomed into a seedling and powerful intoxicants like sunshine and fresh air were pulsing into the budding plant with abundant energy, intensity, and urgency. The kiss that had been shared became equally intoxicating; the relationship, so nourishing in the face of the void that felt so stark and empty.

At which point had the wife betrayed her value of fidelity? Should she never have had lunch with her colleague in the first place? Should they have stopped their meetings when they realized they enjoyed each other's company, even though it just seemed like a friendship? Was the first hug the defining moment, even though it felt like a typical hug from a friend? Was it the tenth hug, the one where she felt the tingling insurgence of attraction? Was it the slip-up of letting themselves flow into a kiss? Or was it what happened after the kiss?

The line becomes blurry. It can be difficult to know when exactly she violated her value of fidelity. The violation was not an explicit, defining moment like taking the bread. There were gradual infringements that seemed innocuous enough in and of themselves, but which actually made the next level of infringement that much more accessible and imminent. All of a sudden, the line is crossed, and the woman feels ashamed and appalled that she's allowed herself to get to that point. Yet, she is also intoxicated by how her lover makes her feel.

An outside observer might think: "Why did you behave that way? There was nothing so wrong or stressful about your environment that it would cause you to behave so uncharacteristically! Your actions, then, must be a true reflection of your poor values. You are not who we thought you were."

We become more inclined to judge and less inclined to offer grace because we can't clearly see, categorize, or understand her context. As an outsider, we probably wouldn't see her multitude of failed attempts to engage her husband, her feelings of marital neglect, or the gradual, almost imperceptible shifts that happened between her and her colleague; we only see the breach of infidelity. We can clearly see that she has crossed the line, yet we have no visibility into the context that led to such an infraction. As such, we conclude that her actions must be a reflection of her true character or values. Again,

---

Replace judgment with curiosity.

The difference between subtle versus overt circumstances can also be applied to cases of emotional and physical abuse.

It is easy to see that physical abuse is an explicit violation of healthy boundaries. One partner gets pushed, slapped, overpowered, or touched inappropriately. There is a defining moment. As such, an outsider might look at the incident and immediately understand why the victim then has an uncharacteristic, stress-induced response (perhaps they punched back, drained funds from the bank account out of fear, or left the marriage). This is not something the victim otherwise would have desired for themselves, chosen to do, or supported in principle, but they acted out of duress in a given set of circumstances.

With emotional abuse, it is often more gradual and harder to identify (for outsiders, for the victim, and even sometimes for the perpetrator). There is no defining moment like a punch to the face. There is no physical sign—no black eye, no bruises, no scratches—to indicate explicit abuse. For outsiders looking in, it may be difficult to understand why the victim of the abuse may have resorted to punching their partner, draining the funds, or leaving the marriage.

An example of this type of subtle abuse, which occurs quite frequently in struggling relationships, is gaslighting. Gaslighting causes extreme amounts of instability, uncertainty, and duress for the victim yet, by its very nature, is difficult to identify.

> The term [gaslighting] originates in the systematic psychological manipulation of a victim by her husband in the 1938 stage play *Gas Light*. [...] In the story, the husband attempts to convince his wife and others that she is insane by manipulating small elements of their environment and insisting that she is mistaken, remembering things incorrectly, or delusional when she points out these changes. The play's title alludes to how the abusive husband slowly dims the gas lights in their home, while pretending nothing has changed, in an effort to make his wife doubt her own perceptions. The wife repeatedly asks her husband to confirm her perceptions about the dimming lights, [...] but in defiance of reality, he keeps insisting that the lights are the same and instead it is she who is going insane.[2]

Whenever one person is continually made to question their judgment, memory, or perception of reality and the other person remains insistent upon theirs, gaslighting is typically present. The victim often defers more and more to the gaslighter in order to avoid conflict and maintain peace between them. This is how the perpetrator gains control. This dangerous phenomenon is insidious not only because it is hard to identify, but also because the perpetrator may not even intend to be doing it. It can even happen between two people who seem to get along.

The shifts are so gradual that the victim often doesn't even realize they're being abused until something jolts them into awareness and they look back, shocked by the extent and duration of the emotional abuse. Since there is no single point at which the perpetrator clearly crossed the line, it becomes harder to understand why the victim may have responded in an uncharacteristic way (punching their partner, draining the funds in fear, or leaving the marriage).

Even though it is harder to identify the circumstances, the victim may still be under extreme duress and behave uncharacteristically. You cannot fully know what's going on for them.

Practice Curiosity

If you have been let down by your partner's actions and feel like they no longer share the same values you thought they had, try to open your perspective and consider their circumstances. In all likelihood, it's not necessarily that their core values have changed, it's rather that their internal state has become so painful that the need to change eclipses their core value.

> *"We change our behavior when the pain of staying the same becomes greater than the pain of changing."*
> —Henry Cloud

By considering that they might still hold this core value, you can then start to get curious about their painful context. This helps you cultivate a more peaceful heart toward your partner because you soften the judgmental story you were telling yourself about their character—the one you had believed was true and complete.

When you find yourself in judgment, reflect instead upon questions that invoke curiosity:

- What might be going on for your partner?

- What internal battle has become so intense that they are choosing to act in a way that contradicts their once-professed, dearly held values?

- Has the fear of financial instability become so strong that they work lots of overtime, despite their value of being family oriented? Or, despite this value of being family oriented, might they be feeling unappreciated and unrecognized and, hence, decide to pour themselves into their work in order to achieve success and feel important?

- Has the pain of emotional disconnection become so great that their desperation to be loved and appreciated by someone drives them to the arms of someone else, despite their value of fidelity?

- Has their exhaustion become so extreme that they can't find the motivation to get up off the couch and play with the kids, even though they value having a strong relationship with them?

- Has the need to control some aspect of their lives become so strong that the only thing they feel they can control is the food they put in their mouth, so despite the value they place on physical health, they become bulimic or anorexic?

It is easy to judge the resulting action and assume your partner no longer holds the value they've acted against. The action is, after all, the most blatant and visible part of the equation. Yet, in all probability, there is a lot going on beneath the surface that is harder to identify and is causing them internal friction, creating a dissonance so strong that their core value is overshadowed by this more pressing need or desire. This dissonance is hard to identify. It is less visible, less defined, and less objective than an explicit action and yet is still extremely powerful and influential for them.

If you find yourself in judgment of your partner, courageously step out of that judgment (if even just for a moment) and get curious about your partner's context. Consider their emotional state, their circumstances, their needs, their fears, and their desires, as well as other affecting factors you might know nothing about. You will not know what exactly is affecting them, but simply by being curious about it you can begin to see them with more humanity.

Or perhaps it was not your *partner* who erred, but *you*. Perhaps *you* made choices that contradict your long-held values and *you* are struggling to understand why and how that happened. This process of replacing judgment with curiosity is also applicable and helpful for your own introspection.

During divorce and in the lead-up to divorce, it is not uncommon for people to be feeling such acute pain that they behave in ways that are uncharacteristic. Perhaps these are explicit behaviors like an affair or perhaps they are more subtle behaviors like withdrawing from the relationship and disengaging from their partner. Either way, these are times of intense pain and confusion, when the world feels like it's topsy-turvy.

Try to give your partner (and yourself) grace and understanding during this time. Choices that one or both of you are making may not be characteristic of who you are or of the choices you would typically make in more "normal," stable circumstances.

Consider Their Circumstance, Not Their Character

We have seen how this concept of "consider their circumstance, not their character" can be helpful in both subtle and overt situations of duress. Surprisingly, it is just as pertinent in times of relative stability as it is in times of duress. Even in innocuous circumstances, when we are irritated with someone, we tend to judge their character.

For example, when you get cut off on the freeway, you might call that person an idiot, a reckless driver, or a "typical female driver." When your spouse lounges on the couch all morning, you may think they're lazy, irresponsible, or unmotivated. Or, when your spouse leaves clothes on the floor, you might think they're slobby. We all do it, in big ways and small.

What's interesting is that when you find *yourself* in the same situation—when it's *you* who cuts someone off on the freeway, binge-watches Netflix, or leaves clothes on the floor—you probably blame it on your *circumstance*: "I know I'm driving fast, but I'm late getting the kids from school," "I'm binge-watching because I've had such an exhausting week," or "I'm so tired I'll just pick up my laundry in the morning."

Notice that we tend to *blame our circumstance*, but in the same scenario we *judge our partner's character*.

When we blame the circumstance,
we continue to have respect for the person.
When we judge their character,
we lose respect for that person.

Unfortunately, we typically do not grant our partners the same grace we grant ourselves. Instead, we judge their character and the infraction becomes a reflection of who they are. The destructive seeds of cynicism and superiority are thus planted.

This is not to say that the behavior, annoying as it is, should go unaddressed. On the contrary, if something about your partner's behavior is bothering you (like lying on the couch all morning), you should address it. But first, get yourself out of judgment in one of two ways:

- Either connect to that trait in yourself:

    Recall a time when you yourself were also that way. Think to yourself, "When was the last time *I* was lazy?" Maybe it wasn't the same action—maybe you weren't sitting on the couch for hours—but there have undoubtedly been times when you were lazy. Perhaps it was last month when you took that hour-long bath, or last week when you left the dishes in the sink overnight. This helps you understand that you also exhibit that same trait sometimes and perhaps you shouldn't judge the other person so harshly for being that way.

- Or attribute their behavior to their circumstance:

    Just as you would blame your laziness on your circumstance ("I had a hard week, so I'm taking a long bath"), get curious about your *partner's* circumstance. Keep in mind that you can never know the full scope of what they are dealing with; circumstances are not always what they seem. Even if you cannot identify the extenuating circumstances, you can simply acknowledge that there may be more going on than what you can see. This alone can help soften your judgment.

Taking a moment to calm your judgment using either of these techniques will help you to approach your partner with less cynicism and superiority, and instead pave the way for a more productive interaction together. It's not to say your partner is not a lazy slob (perhaps they are!), but by stepping out of this initial character judgment, you take a more open approach and set yourselves up for a productive exchange.

The situation can now be used as an opportunity for learning, communication, and perhaps even increased intimacy. You become more familiar with what's affecting your partner (they've had a hard week, they're worried about something, they feel like expectations are too high, etc.) and you have the opportunity to share with your partner about why it matters to you (you're longing to spend time together, having a clean home makes you feel more relaxed, etc.).

When there is an irritating behavior that needs addressing, it doesn't mean your partner necessarily did something *wrong* (or that *you* are wrong to be annoyed by it). It simply means that something is out of alignment between the two of you and it needs addressing.

Not only does this tendency to judge your partner's character come into play during a divorce, but it also tends to get magnified exponentially. When something happens, you automatically interpret it as a shortcoming or fault of theirs. It becomes a reflection of who they are as a person and it affirms you've made the right decision in divorcing. Instead, open your heart by getting curious about their situation: What might they be going through or dealing with at the moment? Are they overwhelmed with uncertainty, pain, fear, or other emotions that are influencing their actions?

Show your former partner the same amount of grace that you grant yourself:

*Consider their circumstance instead of
blaming their character.*

The False Dichotomy of "Either/Or"

We will continue to explore these concepts using the scenario of infidelity, since it is one of the most wounding experiences a couple can go through. The concepts are applicable regardless of how dramatic or intense the scenario. If you can apply them to something as deep and tumultuous as infidelity, you will be able to apply them in most other situations as well.

In the scenario of infidelity, the concept of reframing "either/ or" into "both/and" can be particularly tender.

There are many articles and books out there that support the perspective of the betrayed partner. This side of the story is well understood, well documented, and easy to rally behind. Less talked about, however, is a more even-tempered look at the unfaithful partner's struggle. Let's explore this—not with the goal of convincing you to change your values or loosen your boundaries, but rather to challenge the rigidity of beliefs you might hold about those who have engaged in adultery.

If your husband has betrayed you, you will understandably lose an enormous amount of trust in him. You will be skeptical about believing the things he says. You will second-guess his explanations and his stories. Whenever there are explanations that seem to not match, this will provide further "evidence" that he is a liar and cannot be trusted.

In situations of betrayal, common questions are posed such as "Do you love her...or me?" "Do you want to stay married?" "Are you sorry for what you did?" "Can you promise to be faithful from here on out?" and "Will you do whatever it takes to make it up to me so that I can rebuild trust in you?"

These questions are posed in earnest; however, they are a double-edged sword and are rarely productive. This is because the betrayed spouse is usually looking for an "either/or" answer:

- Either you love her…or me.

- Either you're sorry…or you're not.

- Either you'll do whatever it takes to make this marriage work…or you won't.

They are extremely difficult to answer (for either partner) because if the individual is answering honestly, it's not usually an all-or-nothing, black-and-white, straightforward answer. It's shades of gray: both answers feel true in different ways, to varying degrees, and at various times throughout the day. Instead of an "either/or" answer, the truthful answer would usually take the form of "both/and," which can feel like a conundrum for our categorization-driven brains.

When a wife asks, "Do you love her…or me?" the truthful answer is often, "Both: I love her…*and* I love you." From the perspective of the betrayed, this answer doesn't make sense. It is incomprehensible and reinforces her opinion that her partner is an untrustworthy, dodgy liar, incapable of giving an honest answer. His answer seems inconsistent, invalid, and incomprehensible—it creates cognitive dissonance in her brain, which is distressing. In order to resolve this dissonance, she will likely assume that it cannot be true and that her partner is lying.

Yet, from the perspective of the betrayer, the answer can feel completely true. If he were giving a more robust, explicit answer, it might be: "I love you both in different ways. I love how I feel when I'm with her. I love the starry-eyed way she looks at me and the strong attraction we feel together; I love how passionate sex is with her; and I love how she listens deeply and cares about my day. With you, I feel like those things aren't present and I miss them. But I *do* love you. I love that you're my wife, I love how you take such beautiful care of our children, I love the life we've created together, I love the memories we've made together, I love our family, and I love doing things with you like going on vacation or sitting on the couch watching our favorite shows together."

There are many nuances to love, many different ways of experiencing love, and many stages of love. Just as there are more than 200 words for "rain" in Hawaiian, so could we describe 200 nuances of "love." Asking "Do you love her or me?" is a very broad question that could have many nuances, some more hurtful than others. Furthermore, love does not have limited capacity: You can love your first child and still have abundant capacity to love your subsequent children. Similarly, you can deeply love your wife, while also feeling love/attraction/desire for another woman (incompatible as this may seem, it is possible).

These are nuances that, if explored, could help our brains resolve the cognitive dissonance we are trying to resolve when asking simplistic questions and defaulting into an "either/or" way of thinking.

Could the "both/and" scenario be true? Could it be true, in any way, that "my partner is in love with somebody else *and* in love with me"?

The hurt spouse is aching for a solid, simple answer (again, because this eases the brain's process and makes it easier to categorize and decide upon a course of action). Yet, asking or answering the question in such a black-and-white way deprives the couple of the opportunity to know each other (and the situation) more fully.

More often than not, the reality is that things are not black-and-white. Try to open your perspective and explore the shades of gray—the "both/and." You will understand yourselves, each other, and your situation much more fully if you can open your heart and mind to this perspective.

Truths Are Not Static

Not only are the honest answers usually much more complex than a simple answer, they can also shift moment by moment.

When reeling from infidelity, both partners find themselves in the midst of constant flux and emotional upheaval. One day, perhaps they want to salvage their marriage; the next day, they might be convinced divorce is the only option. It is likely that neither have a clear vision of what they want. Neither probably trusts the other. Both are hemorrhaging in pain.

Perhaps the betrayer desperately pleads, "I love you and want to be with you—please work on this with me!" but then a little later is questioned about whether they love their affair partner and the answer is yes. One answer seems to contradict the other in the eyes of the betrayed; they experience cognitive dissonance and it reinforces their belief that their spouse is, indeed, a liar.

Just because truths seem to change,
it does not mean they are lies.

Perhaps one morning you are irate, triggered, and desperately hurting, so you want a divorce. In this moment, this is your authentic truth. A few hours later, you might have a heartfelt conversation with your partner; you feel heard and seen in some small way and this reorients you toward connection, offering a glimmer of hope. In this moment, then, your truth might be that you prefer to salvage your marriage. Your truth now seems different than it was earlier in the day. It's not that you are lying or fickle; it's just that your authentic understanding of what it is you want and need is changing as the circumstances and your interactions together change.

This scenario happened recently with a client of mine who had just discovered her wife had cheated on her. As my client shared their recent conversation, her anger was palpable and she could hardly contain herself. Time after time, she recounted how her wife would say one thing one moment and something that seemed to be contradictory the next. She was beside herself in anger, appalled that her spouse could advertently lie so consistently and unabashedly to her face.

I challenged her on it, saying: "Isn't it possible that, just as *your* feelings are changing day to day, hers might be as well? Don't you authentically want to stay with her and make it work one moment, only to then find yourself convinced you should divorce the next? If you want her to be honest with you, you need to make it *possible* for her to be honest in her messiness—you need to accept that her answer might be changing moment to moment, just as yours is. You need to accept that she is confused and trying to figure out her truth, just as you are. If, with every fluctuation, you accuse her of being a liar, she will shut down—protecting her identity from further accusations—and you won't be able to continue your conversations."

Allow your partner (and yourself) to have fluctuating truths, fluctuating experiences, and fluctuating feelings. If there is one predictable part of divorce, it is that thoughts, feelings, and actions are unpredictable. The more you can release the need for a definitive, easy-to-understand, up-front answer, the more deeply you can explore the context you both are working in. If you can let your respective thoughts and feelings evolve as the context unfolds (without having your character attacked), you can more authentically explore your truths and make well-thought-out decisions together, seeing all the shades of gray.*

---

*If you are still married and are trying to rebuild your relationship after something as devastating as an affair, there are bottom-line agreements that absolutely need to be put in place in order to provide some assurance and scaffolding for healing and recovery. Commit to deciding on these together, to practicing radical honesty, to honoring each other in words and actions, and to being impeccable with your word by adhering to what you jointly decide.

When we look for definitive answers and explanations up front, we often find they are elusive and incomplete. When we struggle to put things into a box, we limit the ever-changing nature of our human experience.

Our truth evolves as we evolve. Our beliefs, reactions, responses, and framework change as we go through life. Our definitions of hard-and-fast, right-and-wrong lines might become a little more blurred as we take into consideration our circumstances and witness firsthand the struggles of others. By virtue of experiencing more of our humanity, our perspectives broaden and our lines soften. That is not to say that our foundational truths and beliefs are completely upended, but they do become more nuanced as we mature and evolve through life.

Interpretation Is Everything

This concept of "both/and" instead of "either/or" is applicable not only in extreme examples such as infidelity, but also in more subtle circumstances such as marital disconnect, which actually accounts for the majority of divorces. In fact, "in probably the most reliable survey ever done on divorce, [...] 80% of divorced men and women said their marriage broke up because they gradually grew apart and lost sense of closeness, or because they did not feel loved or appreciated. Only 20–27% of couples said an extramarital affair was even partially to blame."[3]

As evidenced by this statistic, disconnect is a pernicious killer. It sneaks up on you before you realize how present it is. In these situations, couples gradually grow apart and find themselves experiencing negative sentiment override: When neutral things happen, one or both people interpret it as negative, not neutral. In the beginning of their relationship, they would have undoubtedly let the incident pass without remark. Now, it sticks out in their mind as a negative interaction and a tick against their relationship.

This happens because we are biologically wired to pay keen attention to whatever might be threatening our security and safety—it's our body's way of staying alert to danger and protecting our homeostatic state of being. If you start to feel disconnected from your partner and scared for your future together, your body's radar goes on high alert for any example of behaviors, interactions, or situations that confirm this fear that your future may be in jeopardy. These threats could be emotional, physical, sexual, financial, differences in parenting techniques, or many other aspects of your relationship. Each time you notice something that supports your fear, your mind says, "Ah-ha! I thought so! The risk is real!" It calls your attention to anything that might prove there is instability in your relationship and for your family.

But what you are doing in these instances is looking for examples that reinforce the current story you're telling yourself! If you told yourself another story (like you are still deeply connected, despite your busy lives), you would key into the moments that confirm *that* story. This is called cognitive bias—you tend to notice examples that confirm your current beliefs.

If your husband spends a few months working late at night, you might easily flip into thinking, "He doesn't care about spending time with the family. He's becoming less interested in us and less committed to creating a connected family life together." That thought begins subtly enough, but each time your husband works late, the thought is increasingly reinforced, to the point that it appears to be the indisputable truth.

To counteract these negative sentiment override and cognitive bias tendencies, it helps to notice the distinction between the observing eye and the perceiving eye.

The Observing Eye and the Perceiving Eye

Ryan Holiday shares in *The Daily Stoic* how "the samurai swords-man Musashi made a distinction between our 'perceiving eye' and our 'observing eye.' The observing eye sees what is. The perceiving eye sees what things supposedly mean."[4]

He also points out wisdom from the Greek Stoic philosopher and once-slave Epictetus:

"It isn't events themselves that disturb people,
but only their judgments about them."

Indeed, the event itself is simply that: an event. What we choose to make of the event is up to us.

In other words, imagine we record an incident with a video camera and then replay the recording. It would show us the incident as it occurred, without added emotion, without story attached, and without interpretation. It is simply the sequence of events.

But when we actually *live* these events—or even watch them unfold—we continually create stories for ourselves about what the events mean, how they reflect on us, and how they impact us.

The fabrication of the story is where
divergent truths emerge.

One event. Two people. Two different experiences. Two stories. It's inevitable. Both experiences are valid—and both feel equally true to the respective individuals.

When something happens between the two of you, both of you are going to have different reactions to it. Just as your reaction feels valid and justified, so does theirs. It does not mean one person is right or wrong; you are both simply experiencing things differently.

In order to cultivate a more peaceful heart during divorce, you need to stop judging your partner. Neither of your experiences are more right or wrong than the other's; they are just different (remember "replace judgment with curiosity"?). When you judge your partner, you intrinsically start to feel superior which, in turn, makes you discount their story and give false weight to your own.

Especially during divorce, you need some level of acknowledgement that your former partner is, at least in some ways, still a reasonable human being.* It's easy to slip into judgment and feel like they've become some psychopathic nutjob who needs major counseling, or at least that they've suddenly become nasty and vengeful. It is, of course, very plausible that they are sometimes *behaving* like this, but it doesn't mean they have become some new person (so unlike the one you married) or that their reactions and responses are not valid.

To fully embrace this perspective (that your experience of something is just as valid as your partner's experience of it, even if they seem incompatible), you can begin by distilling the event down to what objectively happened: What is it that a video camera would have shown? What is it that an unbiased person would recount? This is the observing eye. It watches things exactly as they happen—objectively—through the lens of a video camera. For example, it may observe that your husband works late night after night. End of story. No interpretation. Just observation.

Typically, you would almost instantly begin interpreting it. You make up a story about what it means, how it reflects on you, and how it will impact you. This is the perceiving eye and it's this eye that creates the damage.

---

*Of course, there are exceptions. Some people really are abusive or mentally unstable, but these cases are not the majority.

The perceiving eye sees your husband working late every night and translates that into, "He's coming home late night after night. Is he not as interested in us anymore? I thought he cared about spending time with the family. He must not care as much about spending time with us as I thought!" And remember, since your brain is in negative sentiment override, looking out for risks and protecting what you value (like a stable family life), it is hyper-aware of anything that threatens that value. Each time your husband comes home late, your brain interprets that as a confirmation of your suspicion that he no longer cares as much about the family. Your interpretation is, little by little, becoming the Truth with a capital *T*. It no longer seems like a distant possibility—you now see it as the indisputable Truth.

In order to short-circuit your perceiving eye, first begin to notice its presence as often as you can. Then, using a particular event, distill it down and objectively recount what happened. Notice the story you made up about it and imagine various stories your partner might have made up about it (granted, you won't know what story the other person made up about it, but you could at least imagine some possible stories from their perspective). How did each person think and feel as that experience panned out?

A great practice for this is to first identify what it is you're actually perceiving by filling in the blank: "The story I'm making up about this is _____." (This "story" is what the perceiving eye has made up.) Now, take some of the potency away from the perceiving eye by asking yourself, "What other stories could I make up about this?"

For example, when your husband comes home late *again*, notice this with your observing eye and then ask yourself, "What story am I making up about this?" Perhaps your story is: "He must not care as much about spending time with the family as I thought." Call this out as the interpretation of your perceiving eye: "Ah-ha! That's the story I'm making up about it! What are other possible stories?

Maybe his boss has been riding him at work. Maybe he feels like we don't have enough money, so he has to work overtime. Maybe it's more relaxing for him to be at work than here in the chaos... or...I don't know...maybe he is playing long, rousing games of ping-pong with a colleague after everyone else leaves the office!"

You really don't know what the actuality is, and there are a multitude of stories you could make up about it. The key is to notice that your story is simply that: your story. It could be true, it could be false, or it could be a little of both. You just don't know. By noticing that it's merely the story of your perceiving eye, however, it takes away your story's absolute claim to Truth and puts it back in its rightful place, as *a possible explanation* of what's going on.

If you find yourself feeling like your story absolutely has to be the Truth—if it's difficult to even entertain the possibility of there being other stories—start by shifting your statement from "either/ or" to "both/and": Instead of thinking, "My husband is working late every night, so he must not care as much about spending time with the family," rephrase it as: "My husband is working late every night AND he cares a lot about spending time with the family." Even just reframing it as a "both/and" scenario invites a certain amount of curiosity into the space.

Perhaps you find yourself then posing questions such as:

- I wonder if he feels like he's spending enough quality time with us?

- If he does miss spending more time with us, I wonder what it is that's pulling him so strongly toward work? (Or, to the contrary, what's making it difficult for him to be at home?)

- I wonder how he sees this?

- If he's frustrated too, I wonder what he would need in order to feel more work-life balance?

- I wonder what he's hesitant to share with me?

As you can see, this practice of separating the observing eye from the perceiving eye does not give you an answer; in fact, it can feel like it's taking answers away! (After all, you still don't know what his coming home late means and now, you can't even rely on your fabricated explanation for it.) It is extremely useful, however, because it takes the power away from your perceiving eye and puts it back in its rightful place: with the observing eye. The story you were telling yourself gets demoted from "Truth" status to "possibility" status.

This process helps you to open your heart and mind instead of boxing yourself in with the foregone conclusions and cognitive biases that lead to disconnection. It invites curiosity, which ultimately leads to understanding and connection. Simply by recognizing your perceiving eye and challenging its default story, you shift your underlying attitude from one of judgment, fear, blame, and aggression to one of curiosity and recognition that you are both different people with different (valid) experiences.

This practice is all about training your brain to recognize and override your destructive (and very human) tendency of making up a story and then clinging to that story as truth. It can be transformational both during divorce and in how you live life in general.

Sometimes you may be able to engage with your partner and question them about how they see things. However, it is just as effective for you to go through this process internally, without engaging your partner. The very act of asking yourself, "What story am I making up about this?" will help you replace judgment with curiosity and cultivate a more peaceful heart.

Judgment breeds disconnection and contempt;
curiosity breeds connection and understanding.

Clinging to Your Perception as Universal Truth

Catching yourself in your story can be tricky, particularly in the context of divorce. Emotions are raw, hurts are deep, egos are wounded, and the path forward is uncertain. In such unsteady times, we are hungry for stability and cling desperately onto anything that seems sure. Unfortunately, the thing that feels sure is often our negative judgments of people and events, which perpetuates disconnection and contempt.

Sharon Salzberg, co-founder of the Insight Meditation Society, explains:

> Each person's view of events is conditioned by so many things, but when we become afraid or uncertain, we tend to cling to our perceptions as if they were universally true. We confuse the direct nature of an experience with our particular reaction, as though that reaction were mandated by the experience itself. Thus, the world suddenly becomes very small. This is called fixation. When we imagine that all other people are perceiving the world just as we are, or that they should be, we not only reinforce our subjective perceptions but also lose the capacity to connect intimately with others, and we deny the richness of their experiences.[5]

This is particularly important to understand if you will have an ongoing relationship with your partner (as co-parents or in some other form). Even if you are completely parting ways, however, recognizing this tendency can completely shift how you think back about your former partner and this experience years from now.

With this concept of fixation, we find ourselves again in the false pretense of duality—our brains want to classify events into being labeled as one way or the other, automatically discounting the possibility that multiple perspectives could simultaneously be true.

When our version of an event feels absolutely reasonable and justified, it resonates for us as being true. And since our brains tend to see things as either/or, we assume that there is just one truth—ours—and that anything else must not be the truth.

Think about any trivial situation: Say you and a friend both order a caramel latte at your local coffee shop. You think it is the best drink you've had all month, perfectly prepared! Your friend thinks it is too sweet and sends it back. Same coffee, different experiences. In another scenario, suppose you watch the Rose Parade with your husband. You notice the wide variety of flowers and the texture on the floats; your husband notices the celebrities and cheerleaders marching by and misses the nuanced texture of the flowers. Same parade, different experiences.

Likewise in the context of relationship. My husband and I separated when our oldest was six years old and our twins were four. I had been a stay-at-home mom since the twins were born. We had been living outside the United States for five years prior to their birth, so I had not worked in the U.S. for ten years by the time we separated. The year before our separation, I started training as a life coach, which resonated deeply with me as a new direction for my career. After separating, I had to decide whether to continue my education in this new path and take the riskier route of building my own business or return to a 9-to-5 job, where my kids would suddenly be thrown into childcare and my income would be at a professional entry level. I decided to take the time to continue my new career trajectory. For my former partner, it was frustrating and irritating that I opted not to return to my former career and begin making money more quickly. For me, pursuing a resonant career path after having been out of the workforce for so long felt like a valid decision. One situation, two valid experiences.

Learning to hold this paradigm—that one person's experience and truth is as valid as another's—can be transformational in your ability to cultivate a peaceful heart because you develop the ability to accept and meet your partner where they are. In this case, I could understand my former partner's perspective and frustration without being angry at him for having it. At the same time, I was able to remain confident that my choices were supporting my path and my priorities.

You might not *agree* with how your partner is experiencing something or the choices they make, yet you are willing to recognize that their experience is valid and true for them, foreign and unfounded as it may seem to you.

Don't Blame—Seek to Understand How You Both Contributed

When we are frustrated, let down, angry, and hurt, it's common to blame someone else for doing or saying something that caused us to feel this way.

Look at the problems that contributed to your divorce. What story are you telling yourself (and others) about why you are divorcing?

- We are divorcing because she had an affair.

- We are divorcing because he wasn't engaged with the family.

- We are divorcing because she cares about her extended family more than she cares about us.

- We are divorcing because she stopped caring about me.

- We are divorcing because he won't work on the marriage with me.

Or, perhaps you have already divorced and you are trying to sort out the legal issues or continue parenting together. Then your dialogue may be more like this:

- We could co-parent better if only she would actually respond to my texts.

- We would be finished going to court if only he wasn't being so selfish about money.

- We would have a better relationship now if she wasn't so sarcastic every time she spoke to me.

- We could put this whole thing behind us if only he would man up and do his part.

In such a divisive environment, it is easy to point fingers and place the blame on the explicit things your partner is doing "wrong." It feels great to know that it is mostly your partner's fault and that you, on the other hand, are a reasonable, levelheaded person who is mature enough to engage productively. Now, if only your partner would do the same!

When you blame your partner, it reinforces the idea that you made the right decision to not stay married to such a selfish/irresponsible/lazy/unfaithful/(fill-in-the-blank) person. It adds fuel to your fire of resentment, frustration, and indignation. It preserves your narrative, bolsters your ego, protects the image you have of yourself, and relieves you of the need to do any painful introspection about what *you* did to contribute to the situation. It is automatic armor.

Of course, when you point fingers and blame someone, there is indeed a finger pointed at them—they *did* contribute to this mess. But, there are also three fingers pointed back at you—*you also contributed.*

If you're going to weaken the fire of anger in service of cultivating a more peaceful heart, you must also look at how *you* contributed to the situation.

As we saw earlier, the majority of divorces are not the result of an explicit infraction like an affair, physical abuse, irresponsible squandering of finances, or a drug, alcohol, or pornography addiction. Rather, the separation usually happens because the partners gradually grow apart and lose a sense of closeness, or don't feel loved or appreciated. This loss of love and connection, however, is often what creates the context for larger infractions like affairs, depression, and addiction.

When these more explicit infractions happen, it can be particularly tempting to place blame on the offending partner. After all, these infractions can easily be pointed to as blatant evidence that the line of acceptability has been crossed—that the fundamental, bottom-line values you both agreed on are no longer being respected, and that you are therefore warranted in your decision to divorce.

Regardless of whether your fallout is due to subtle or explicit behavior, it is rarely (if ever) all one person's fault (this equally pertains to any disagreement, not just divorce). That is not to say that each person contributed *equally*, but each person *did* contribute. Contributions to a problem can take many forms; oftentimes, it is what someone did or said that creates problems, but it also frequently includes things a person *did not do or say*.

If you are feeling like your spouse was primarily to blame for your separation, ask yourself questions such as:

- What could I have said early on that may have helped us identify this issue and work through it together?
- In what ways could I have been more supportive?
- How could I have held more firmly to my boundaries so that this situation didn't get out of hand?

- ◆ How could I have more clearly stated what was bothering me?

- ◆ What did I *not* do that contributed to this problem? (For example: I didn't go back to work, I didn't wait to eat dinner with her when she came home late, I didn't make time for us after the kids went to bed, I didn't give her enough space to develop friendships, I didn't express my appreciation of him as much as I could have.)

Sometimes the things you *did not* do or say are harder to identify but may have just as much impact on the overall problem.

In order to cultivate a more peaceful heart, you must step away from blame and begin to understand the whole context—which includes your respective contributions to the mess. When you recognize and acknowledge your part in perpetuating the problem, it douses the flames of anger and begins to soften your heart.

Therefore, instead of blaming, look to understand how each person contributed to the situation.

Your Partner Does Not "Make" You Feel a Certain Way

When your partner does something that leaves you feeling hurt, disappointed, frustrated, or angry, it's easy to reactively accuse them of doing something "wrong" and of making you feel this way.

First of all, let's be clear: They did not "make" you feel this way. They did something and you had an emotional response to it. There are actually a range of emotional responses that could be possible, given the same perpetuating event.

Let's consider a situation that commonly causes irritation for couples: doing the dishes. If your partner leaves the dishes in the sink, you might feel really angry ("Argh!! They did it again! We *just* talked about this!"). Perhaps you even feel disrespected—after all, they know it bugs you and yet, they keep doing it.

The perpetuating event is that your partner left the dishes in the sink. Pure and simple. It's the objective event, as witnessed by the observing eye; it's what would be recorded by the video camera.

What are your possible reactions? Anger that it happened, yet again? Frustration that your partner doesn't seem to be hearing your repeated requests? Disappointment that they don't seem to follow through with what they say they'll do?

These feelings are probably the most common and are all somewhat related, so let's challenge your framework of thinking and explore the possible feelings and reactions that are on the other end of the spectrum.

- You could feel compassion: compassion for the fact that your partner has had a long day (yet again).

- You could feel camaraderie and approach your partner with the suggestion, "I know we're both tired. Let's do them together and use this time to connect with each other. We're in this together, you know."

- You could feel empathy, knowing what it's like to feel pressure to do something, even though it's the last thing you feel like doing at that moment.

These thoughts and emotions are probably not the ones that surface by default. In fact, maybe they never surface at all! The point is that these other emotional reactions *are possible*. Your partner did not *make* you angry when they left the dishes in the sink. The anger is yours to own.

How you feel and how you respond
is your responsibility.

When you learn to take personal ownership of how you experience things, you step out of victimhood and into empowered agency. In so doing, your whole world changes.

The Story You Make Up Dictates Your Feelings

If you believe that your feelings are your feelings and that you can't change them—that they're just a natural part of life and are inevitable—it may be useful to look at the relationship between your story and the feelings and actions that follow.

It is your story that dictates your thoughts, your thoughts lead to your feelings, and those feelings inform your actions.

Story

↓

Thoughts

↓

Feelings

↓

Actions

Let's say the two of you are arguing over custody schedules: She wants 80/20 and you want 50/50. Every time you talk about it, she gets riled up, talks to you about how you're not suited to be a 50/50 dad, and threatens that you'll need to prove yourself first before she'll even consider it (which she thinks is unlikely).

It makes you infuriated that she can't see what a good father you are and that she thinks she's more entitled to time with the kids than you are. *Who wouldn't be infuriated? It's natural to feel that way!* you think. *It's obvious she's unreasonable and out for revenge!*

Now, notice your observing eye and your perceiving eye. Ask yourself what, objectively, is going on? And what story are you making up about it?

Your *observing eye* might notice that she's not budging about her position, that she seems passionate about her opinion, and that she comes at you with aggressive words and energy each time you talk with her about it.

Your *perceiving eye* might make up the story that she's grasping for control wherever she can take it and that she wants to punish you for your part in the divorce, making you as miserable through this process as she is. These become your thoughts about her and the situation, and these thoughts evoke a certain set of undesirable feelings (anger, rage, vindication, defensiveness, indignation, etc.). You then respond to her from this place of rage and vindication, which exacerbates the issue, and the unhealthy interaction continues to spiral downward.

If, on the other hand, you stop and notice that the story you're making up is just that—your story—you can start considering other stories that might be true:

- Perhaps she's deeply grieving, thinking about time she'll no longer have with the children if they're with you so much.

- Perhaps she's scared to not have full visibility over what they're taught or how they're raised.

- Perhaps she came from a broken home and had a lot of trouble switching houses, so she wants to minimize that pain for her kids by having one primary home base for them.

- Perhaps she doesn't agree with your religious views or approach to nutrition and cares strongly about surrounding the children with what she considers more healthy approaches.

- Perhaps you have a close friend or relative who is an unhealthy influence on them and she's trying whatever she can to keep the kids away from that person.

The possibilities are endless. You cannot know what is true for her, but simply by considering other possible stories, you open the way for yourself to have different thoughts and feelings. Originally, you felt rage because of the story you were telling yourself: that she wants to punish you for your part in the divorce. If, instead, you consider that she might be behaving like this because she's grieving about the time she'll no longer share with them, you might feel compassion, or at least have a softer heart toward her (which will inevitably change the tone with which you respond to her). Or, if you consider that she might be scared not to have visibility over how they're raised, you might feel more levelheaded and open to discussing with her some parameters around your respective house rules and expectations.

Your story directly influences your thoughts about the situation, your thoughts will affect how you feel, and the way you feel will affect how you speak and behave.

Remember, your brain wants desperately to hold onto its interpretation (in order to classify and understand the situation) and judge your partner (thus protecting yourself, since "they're in the wrong" and "they're to blame"). But it is most often not a black-and-white situation; the situation is made up of shades of gray, there are multiple factors at play, and you have both contributed. By releasing your conviction that your interpretation is the absolute Truth and acknowledging that there are other feasible stories, you will be able to explore other possible thoughts (and thus, other feelings and actions).

The choice is yours in how tightly you choose to cling to your story and which thoughts you choose to have about the event.

Even in extreme situations, we are at choice. Viktor Frankl is a neurologist, psychiatrist, and Holocaust survivor who lived through internments at Theresienstadt, Auschwitz, Kaufering, and Türkheim. Even after having lived through such horrific circumstances, he asserts:

> *"Everything can be taken from a man but one thing: the last of the human freedoms—to choose one's attitude in any given set of circumstances, to choose one's own way."*

Now that you are aware of this tendency to constantly make up stories about what's happening around you, you can diminish the omnipotence of your perceiving eye simply by noticing it. You are now at choice about the story you choose to believe, and this will influence how you feel and act. You now have the skills to take charge of your experience and you are no longer the victim of circumstance.

As pastor and educator Charles Swindoll says, "Life is 10% what happens to you and 90% of how you react to it." The choice is yours: Are you opting to cultivate a bitter, resentful heart, or are you opting to cultivate a more peaceful heart?

You Can Begin Your Healing Now

You might be thinking: *I am so hurt and angry right now! It's all I can do just to get through each day...I don't know how I can even begin to think about cultivating a more peaceful heart right now!*

You can.

You can be hurt and angry AND
have a peaceful heart.

Remember, these two states of being seem opposed, so believing that both can be true simultaneously creates cognitive dissonance. Your brain tries to resolve this dissonance by making you believe that you can *either* be hurt and angry *or* have a peaceful heart, but not both. You therefore conclude that because you know you are so hurt and angry, it must be that you cannot cultivate a more peaceful heart just yet, and that only after your hurt and anger have subsided will a more peaceful heart be possible.

This is not an all-or-nothing process, however. If you wait until you are free of hurt and anger to begin cultivating a peaceful heart, you may be waiting a long time. My former husband and I have been separated for several years, and I have been relatively successful in cultivating a peaceful heart. Yet even now I experience bouts of hurt and anger. Had I waited for the pain and anger to subside, I might still be waiting to begin nurturing a peaceful heart and would have lost out on much of the inner calm I've experienced so far.

If you feel hopelessly weighed down by hurt and anger and find that a peaceful heart seems inaccessible right now, remember that your brain is wired to protect your well-being. By allowing the hurt and anger, your brain thinks it is doing just that: protecting you.

The voice inside your head might be screaming: "She hurt you! You *should* be angry! If you stop being angry and hurt, you might become complacent and forgiving. You need to be strong and stand up for yourself! Don't let her take advantage of you! If you start having a more peaceful heart, you're going to become soft and she'll walk all over you. Give her an inch and she'll take a mile. She deserves it anyway; don't give her any favors."

As we've seen, when you're hurting and upset, blaming your partner feels good; it relieves you of your responsibility (or so you think). It paints the picture that you are innocent, justified, and reasonable and they are at fault. So, given the choice of "either/or," your brain defaults to protection and chooses hurt and anger over a peaceful heart.

The fact is, however, that you *can* have both: You can be hurt and angry, and still cultivate a peaceful heart. Again, you can aspire to this definition of peace:

"Peace. It does not mean to be in a place with no noise, trouble, or hard work. It is to be in the midst of these things and still be calm in your heart."
—*Author unknown*

It bears repeating: The goal is not to eliminate negative feelings and experiences from your path; these are a part of life and ubiquitous in divorce. Rather, it is to give you a path toward gradually opening your heart, building an intrinsic sense of peace, strength, clarity, and confidence that will provide a counterbalance for the intensity of those negative feelings. It will expedite your healing.

The more you focus on shifting your paradigm and integrating these concepts into your heart and mind, the more you will feel at peace.

Setting Sail

Let the ideas of this framework percolate into your subconscious; ponder these new ways of thinking. Try them out, even if it's little by little. Think back on recent experiences and practice applying them—see how they fit and how your attitude toward the event shifts. What opens up for you?

Integrating this framework into your way of thinking about the world will help you broaden your lens from a harsh black-and-white view to a more useful (and accurate) lens of gradients of gray. The more you lean into this framework, the more you can break through past paradigms that restrict your heart and hamper your healing, and the more ease you will have in continuing on this journey of divorce.

With this new foundation of a more open heart, let's now explore the guiding principles—tools that will help you navigate through the storm, keeping your ship upright and your heart peaceful as you go.

Let the wind fill your sails and let the following principles guide you.

You are not the victim of circumstance. You are the leader of your life, the captain of your ship.

Let's do this.

SECTION 2

NAVIGATE THE STORM WITH A PEACEFUL HEART

SET YOUR COMPASS TOWARD THE NORTH STAR OF COMPASSION

 # CAPTAIN'S LOG

"I am navigating through the turbulent waters of separation and divorce. The journey is overwhelming at times—I have been tossed about by the ruthless waves of deep emotion and changing circumstance, often feeling off course, frustrated, overwhelmed, and without a map to guide me. I find ballast through my consciously selected cargo and crew: principles and people that steady my hull and allow me to practice openheartedness while I remain ever-focused on my North Star: Compassion. As such, even in the largest of waves, my ship has remained upright—my hull stable, and my peaceful heart my refuge." —S.M.

Divorce is fraught with many feelings and emotions: blame, hurt, anger, resentment, broken dreams, devastation. It is a total crumbling of who you thought you were and what kind of life you thought you'd lead.

Everything is in upheaval and yet, you have to find a way forward. So many things are in flux: where to live, how this will affect your job, whether to hire lawyers, how the kids are going to fare, and how the assets will be divided.

It's hard to find calibration around what qualifies as "reasonable": In trying to keep the peace, are you actually selling yourself short by not standing up for what is rightfully yours? Is amicability even possible at this point? Are you asking for too much? Is your former spouse?

Everything is shifting. It feels like the ground is falling out from under you—like solid footing is nowhere to be found. You feel seasick, weary, and off-balance, like you're on a ship lost at sea in the middle of a tempest with no navigation system. Tossed by the relentless waves, you are pummeled and thrashed about, with no indication of when this assault is going to end. You are overwhelmed, not knowing where to go, how to proceed forward, or when you're going to get your next breath.

What follows is an in-depth look at five principles that can help you navigate the storm.

The first principle—and primary navigational beacon—is the North Star: *Compassion.* Keeping compassion foremost in your mind will not only help orient you in the midst of your storm, it will also help you successfully cultivate a peaceful heart while you navigate through the turbulent waters.

The subsequent four principles will create ballast,* steadying your hull and offering you peace as you travel through your storm toward calmer waters:

Principle 2: Replace Judgment with Curiosity

Principle 3: Make Self-Respect a Priority

Principle 4: Do Your Best and Let Go of the Rest

Principle 5: Choose Your Crew Wisely

Let the five principles guide you. If all you can handle at this point is one thing, follow the light of *Compassion*. Little by little, as the hemorrhaging slows, you can begin to incorporate the other principles as well.

Go slowly. Don't expect to get it all at once. Read little bits at a time if you are feeling quite raw, or scan through all the principles to begin with and then come back and take a little more time to digest each one. Reread the book as needed—you'll find there are golden nuggets that were not accessible to you initially, but that offer you renewed hope, healing, and richness at this new stage of your journey.

Lean into these principles as you are able; they will help you find your footing and begin your process of healing, even while you are in the thick of the emotional turmoil. In fact, learning to apply these principles early on—while you are still in pain—can have the greatest effect on your overall outcome, recovery, and happiness. By orienting toward these principles in the here and now, you are actively shifting your rudder by small degrees. These small shifts now can make a huge difference in where you end up. Doing it months from now would mean you have already traveled far off

---

*Ballast is heavy material such as gravel, sand, iron, or lead, placed low in a vessel to improve its stability.

course and now need to make up that distance, having incurred unnecessary pain and wasted resources along the way.

"If you don't know where you're going, you'll end up someplace else." —Yogi Berra

---

Set your sights on the North Star of Compassion; let it orient you through your divorce. It may feel extremely challenging to access compassion now, in the midst of the raging storm, but stand firmly at the helm and keep yourself oriented toward that goal.

It is worth noting at this point that having compassion does not mean being weak or being walked all over. Clear boundaries are a necessary partner to compassion and will be addressed in Principle 3. Compassion, however, is the starting point for healing and is thus the guiding star for our journey.

With compassion as your primary beacon, you can cultivate a peaceful heart, even while navigating the hurt, pain, and chaos of divorce.

Why Cultivate a Compassionate Heart?

It is important to be clear about why you are cultivating a compassionate heart.

If you are hoping to shift the chain of events, get back together with your partner, or change the other person in some way, you are inviting disappointment and disillusionment. You may be able to *influence* those things, but *you cannot control them*. You must be doing it for your own growth, liberation, healing, and peace of mind. If your partner softens because of it, fantastic! But you must let go of that hope, letting it be a welcome surprise if it *does* happen.

As with forgiveness, approaching your former partner with a compassionate heart is for your own liberation. As a therapist once said, "Being angry at your ex is like sitting down every day and preparing a glass of poison for them, but then drinking it yourself!"

Nurturing a compassionate, peaceful heart within yourself will allow you to heal from the inside out, and this is possible even as the pain and suffering persist.

Be Compassionate toward Your Former Partner...and Yourself

We all go through struggles at some point and we all deal with them differently. Whether it's divorce or a myriad of other life trials—physical or mental health struggles, career difficulties, strained relationships, natural disasters, or global pandemics—they are part of life. Having struggles doesn't diminish your value as a human being; you are no less worthy of love or happiness.

Challenges in life happen to even the most enlightened humans. Being an evolved, conscious individual who has done a lot of self-work doesn't isolate you from the trials and tribulations of life. You will still experience them! But focusing on your personal growth and cultivating a peaceful heart does give you tools to move through these struggles with more ease and recover from them more quickly and wholly.

Divorce is fraught with upheaval and brings unpredictable times. Some days you might feel well equipped and prepared for what comes your way; other days, you might barely be able to function. During this period, foster compassion for yourself as well as your former partner.

Your best today doesn't look the same as it did yesterday, nor will it be the same in a month. Give yourself wide latitude as you navigate through this time. Let yourself feel sad. Let yourself feel hurt. Let yourself long for something more. Let yourself dream. Let yourself fear. Let yourself experience the range of human emotions. Do not saturate yourself with them, allowing yourself to wallow in them any longer than necessary, but do let yourself feel and experience them. The more you can let these emotions come and go as you go about your daily life, the quicker you will be able to heal.

> *These experiences are transitory.*
> *It will not be like this forever.*

Healing is a process and it will take time. You'll think you have finished grieving and then all of a sudden find yourself deeply affected by something all over again. Part of healing is allowing yourself the space to grieve: grieve the person you once were, grieve the life you thought you were creating, grieve the dreams that have now been broken, grieve the person you thought you'd be, grieve the life you thought you'd be living.

Perhaps one of the hardest aspects to grieve is your changed identity. No longer are you the parent of an intact family; your children are now the children of divorce. No longer are you able to be the stay-at-home mom. No longer do you have time to be the soccer dad or coach for your child's team. No longer do you have a ring on your finger—that cherished symbol of love and belonging.

The Pain of Change

Grief happens because things change; something is lost and life is no longer what you knew it to be. This is also often accompanied by pain, and pain—by its very nature—hurts. But the presence of pain is not always bad: It can also indicate growth. As difficult as it might be to see when you're in the midst of it, the aches you are experiencing now may ultimately be growing pains. You may be in the midst of a beautiful transformation.

Consider the metamorphosis of a caterpillar as it becomes a butterfly. When a caterpillar has reached the end of a particular stage of life, it hardens into a chrysalis and releases an enzyme that literally eats its body up, turning it into a liquid, soupy substance. Over the next few weeks, it completely rebuilds itself from this mush, squeezes its way out of its chrysalis, and becomes a beautiful butterfly. The DNA it needs to become this beautiful being is always present, but the caterpillar has to bring that part of its life to a halt, turn inward, liquify its current self into mush, rebuild while protecting itself, and then work diligently to push through its constricting encasement before entering into its next stage of life.

Divorce often feels like you are being turned to mush—overwhelmed by assaults from your partner, your circumstance, and even the way you are thinking about yourself. This period of breaking down is inevitably followed by a period of building up. You intrinsically have what is needed to transform into a new beautiful version of yourself. Yes, you have changed. Yes, your circumstances are different now. Yes, some dreams have been crushed. Yes, you probably have no idea how life is going to shake out during the next few years. But this is indeed a time of transformation. It is temporary and you will emerge as a wiser, stronger, adapted self. Perhaps this is the beginning of a more fulfilling stage of life—one that would never have been possible without the painful, soupy stage you're going through now.

When you're in the midst of that soupy stage, however, it can be hard to have faith that this might actually be a very positive turning point in your life. For now, you're treading water and just need to figure out how to stay afloat day by day.

Don't "Should" on Yourself

This restructuring of identity can feel like it's taking place at a deep, soul level.

- Perhaps you had always envisioned yourself married, and now find yourself single.

- Perhaps you had always imagined you'd be faithful and true, yet you find yourself as a betrayer.

- Perhaps you had complete confidence in this person you were marrying and have been deeply disappointed in who they've become or how they've behaved.

- Perhaps now you're questioning your ability to choose healthy partners.

- Perhaps you always envisioned being a stable, two-parent household and now that dream has dissolved.

Whatever the case, divorce usually leads to some amount of disintegration of identity—some dream that was, and will now be no more; some label you thought you would never have, but now find yourself with. This reidentification can be extremely painful and rebuilding can feel out of reach, particularly in the beginning.

Allow yourself plenty of space to go through this process; be gentle with yourself and know that this is temporary. You don't need to shift out of it right away. But it will shift. You will find your way out and there will be days where you feel slightly more at ease. Expect yourself to have moments of breakdown. Accept that this will happen and that it is a normal part of the process—it is to be expected.

Set the intent for healing, but don't force it. You'll probably find yourself saying: "I should be healing faster," "I should be finding my way," "I should know what to do," "I should be able to deal with this better."

Don't "should" on yourself.

Notice that this self-talk is present, then allow these chastising thoughts to drift away like the clouds in the sky and replace them with loving self-acceptance. Do not compare yourself to your perceived ideals. Allow yourself to be where you are with ease, grace, and self-compassion.

Calming Your Body and Mind When Stressed or Triggered

During divorce and the period of post-divorce, there is a large amount of uncertainty and instability because things are in a constant state of change. With this change comes the unknown and with the unknown comes fear. For some, it is a very conscious fear. For others, it is more subconscious, yet it still manifests in a certain amount of anxiety, exhaustion, curtness, or stress.

We find ourselves in a state of survival—just trying to hold it together and get through the next day, making the best decisions we can along the way.

Any time your brain thinks your well-being is threatened (whether something feels at risk physically, financially, emotionally, relationally, or otherwise), it goes into high alert. This activates your sympathetic nervous system—otherwise known as your fight-or-flight response. Since you are wired to protect yourself, your fight-or-flight response will activate any time you feel threatened, regardless of whether that threat is real or perceived.

Begin to recognize your tendency: Do you fight? Flee? Freeze? Shut down and escape within? When you notice yourself reacting in these ways, don't judge—you are experiencing a natural response either to stress or to being in a constant state of change and uncertainty. Your status quo feels threatened, and you are wired to respond.

When your fight-or-flight response is activated, blood flows away from your brain and gut toward the muscles needed to fight or get away. Your legs, arms, heart, and lungs become primed and ready for action. Your pupils dilate to gather more information and your brain releases stress hormones, such as cortisol and adrenaline, to keep you on high alert.

These are all extremely helpful responses when you are actually in immediate danger. However, during divorce, our bodies and minds often *interpret* that we are in immediate danger, when in actuality we are not. It feels like we are under almost constant threat (or at least that we are unsafe because of our constantly changing environment).

As these perceived threats typically persist for months or years during a divorce, our stress hormones can easily remain elevated. When sustained over a long period of time, this causes overwhelm, fatigue, sickness, stress, and a reduced capacity to function effectively.

When the threat is acute (say, in the middle of an argument with your spouse where your relationship's future feels threatened, or arguing about child support when your financial well-being feels threatened), the fight-or-flight response takes over and actually inhibits your ability to think clearly and communicate effectively. This phenomenon is known as amygdala hijack.

During amygdala hijack, you cannot think effectively because the amygdala (the emotional response center that is responsible for emotions such as fear and anxiety) is the first to react. It takes control of your brain before your more rational, calm neocortex (which governs your logical thinking and reasoning abilities) can engage. As long as the threat remains present, the amygdala (the fear center) remains in control, essentially taking the neocortex "offline" until the threat subsides.[6] So you literally cannot think straight when you feel threatened. Remember, this threat can be real or perceived, and is not always a physical threat. It can also be threats to your relational, financial, environmental, or family stability. Regardless, when your brain perceives a threat, it kicks into high alert.

The more quickly you can let your body and mind know you are not actually in danger, the more quickly you can calm the response of your limbic system and begin thinking and interacting rationally again. An effective way to do this is through a very simple practice: deep breathing.

Taking a deep breath signals to your body that you are safe. When you are scared or on edge, your breathing becomes shallow and fast (a sympathetic nervous system response). When you take deep breaths, your body relaxes and your parasympathetic nervous system engages. The parasympathetic nervous system is the complement to the sympathetic nervous system; its response is known as the rest-and-digest response (as opposed to fight-or-flight).

During this rest-and-digest phase, blood flows away from the larger muscles of your legs, arms, heart, and lungs and back to your brain and gut. Your pupils go back to normal, your brain stops releasing so much cortisol and adrenaline, and your body resets into a more neutral state. Thankfully, we can engage this part of our nervous system by simply taking a few deep breaths.

Here are three breathing practices you can try. The first two are integrated practices that you can use in the moment whenever you are feeling triggered, and the third is a dedicated practice, which means you practice it by setting aside specific time in your day for it.

Self-Compassion Breathing Mantra (Integrated Practice)

This practice is useful any time you feel frustrated or overwhelmed (for example, while awaiting a court judgment, arguing with your former spouse, dropping your children off with your co-parent when you wished you didn't have to, or just trying to make it through your day).

It takes only five seconds and is comprised of taking one deep, full breath. As you slowly breathe in and out for one full breath cycle, repeat this mantra to yourself:

"I breathe in, I do my best.
I breathe out, I let go of the rest."

When you do this, literally try to feel it in your body:

- As you breathe in, acknowledge your best efforts (don't think about them specifically, but just acknowledge that you are doing your best in this moment).

- As you breathe out, release the tension you physically are holding in your muscles, shoulders, back, and neck. Try to let your soul relax and breathe.

4-5-6 Breathing (Integrated Practice)

This practice is slightly longer, taking approximately one minute. It is useful because it not only relaxes your body in the moment, but also helps train your brain to recognize how deeply renewing and refreshing it is to breathe deeply in the moment. The more often you can train yourself to take slow, deep breaths, the more second nature it will be when you are triggered and really need it.

To do this practice:

- Breathe in for four seconds.
- Hold your breath for five seconds.
- And breathe out for six seconds.
- Repeat this three times, for a total of four breaths.

Do this whenever you like, as a way to get into the habit of taking deep, calming breaths. It can help to associate it with a regular part of your routine so you remember to do it: perhaps every morning while your coffee brews, when you take a shower, or when you turn off the ignition in your car. You can even try putting a Post-it note reminder on your bathroom mirror or making it the screen saver on your phone.

Breathing Meditation (Dedicated Practice)

This practice will take a little more time but can feel as deeply refreshing as a full nap. It can span anywhere from a few minutes to 15 minutes or longer, depending on how long you'd like to spend. You can find timers and guided versions of meditations like this on meditation apps.* They are powerful resources for all levels of meditation practitioners.

During the meditation, you'll probably notice that thoughts are constantly coming and going in your mind. This is completely normal. Don't get down on yourself; don't feel like you're no good at it or doing it wrong. Asking your thoughts to stop completely is like asking your heart to stop beating. Instead of resisting these

---

*Two popular meditation apps today are Headspace and Insight Timer.

thoughts, just notice them when they come and let them gently fade away. Try not to go down the rabbit hole of following those thoughts and letting them meander. Just let them come and go like headlines in a news ticker, scrolling along the bottom of your screen.

When you notice yourself feeling distracted by these thoughts, bring your attention back to your breath. This consistent action of bringing your attention back to your breath when you get distracted is actually an attention-training practice in and of itself.

To do this breathing meditation, set a timer for the time you'd like to spend, then sit with your feet flat on the floor and your back against a chair—alert, but relaxed. As you read, pause after each line, allowing yourself ample time to try each phrase.

> Close your eyes or soften them while you read, and notice where your body feels tense. Breathe into those tense places, inviting them to relax, even just a little bit. As you settle into your chair, gradually turn your attention to your breathing.
>
> Notice the air coming in and out through the tip of your nose. What temperature is the air as it comes in? What temperature is it as it goes out?
>
> Notice the air going through your nose and into your throat and chest.
>
> Notice the rise and fall of your chest, the expansion and release of your rib cage.
>
> Notice your belly moving in and out.
>
> Now expand your awareness to notice your whole breathing system at once. What does it feel like to breathe? What do you notice?

What sensation feels the most prominent while you're breathing? Is it the rise and fall of your chest? Is it the air passing through the tip of your nose?

This prominent sensation will become your anchor point for the rest of the meditation. Whenever your attention drifts, bring your attention gently back to this anchor point.

Spend the rest of your time simply breathing, with your attention placed on that anchor point. When your timer sounds, take one last full breath in and out, then slowly open your eyes.

Wiggle your fingers and toes, and gently come back to the here and now.

Take a quiet moment of gratitude for this time you've carved out for your self-care and healing.

These breathing practices can help calm your mind, body, and spirit when you're feeling threatened or unstable. They sometimes take just moments, but can have tangible, positive effects on your mental, emotional, and physical well-being.

Give Yourself Grace and Understanding

An essential part of navigating divorce with a peaceful heart is learning how to approach both yourself and your former partner with compassion and understanding. Each of you is likely behaving in ways that feel uncharacteristic and negative—ways that you never would have anticipated during the early days of marriage. Both of you are likely acting and reacting from a place of pain, disappointment, and protection.

Just as you give yourself grace, give your partner grace.

By keeping your compass oriented toward the North Star of Compassion and by doing your best to cultivate a peaceful heart during this period, you can hold your head high and ultimately expedite your inner healing, despite the brokenness you're currently feeling. This may feel unattainable right now, but set your sights and intentions there and move in that direction.

As Unity minister Deanna Joseph says:

"Be a love amplifier and a grace generator."

Start with yourself and then practice extending it toward your partner when you are able to access little glimmers of it. It is not an all-or-nothing endeavor: It may be difficult to extend grace toward your former partner when you start. If this is the case, notice when you can muster even a *glimmer* of grace, understanding, or appreciation for them. Then focus on it and magnify it, even if it's by just five percent. Little by little, you will have more of those moments and your foundation will change from being one of anger and revenge to one of strength, clarity, and compassion.

PRINCIPLE 2

REPLACE JUDGMENT
WITH CURIOSITY

 CAPTAIN'S LOG

"The storm continues to rage. It's true that I may not have reacted in the way you are acting, but we are not the same people—you have suffered hurts that I have not; your experiences have not been mine; we have different ways of dealing with stress. I cannot pretend to understand everything that is influencing your behavior right now. You must be doing your best under the circumstances. If you are acting like this, you must be suffering from intense pain...maybe there are wounds from your past that are being scraped open or maybe there are core needs that are unmet; perhaps you haven't learned the tools needed to deal with the level of grief or trauma you're experiencing; perhaps what I am doing or saying is triggering feelings within you that I don't understand.

I remember how I was once in love with you. I chose you, out of everyone else, to be my cherished partner in life. I'm sorry that your hurts run so deeply that you're acting in ways that are uncharacteristic of who I know you are at your core.

As I extend compassion to myself for the choices I have made, so also do I extend it to you. We are both human, doing our best on this journey of life." —S.M.

If Not Compassion, Curiosity

In some cases, the wounding, pain, and abuse run too deep to be able to access compassion. If you find that compassion is just not possible for you to muster at this stage, at least practice curiosity. Again:

Replace judgment with curiosity.

Why might your partner be lashing out? What is it about their past or their mindset that is causing them to act that way? What are they are afraid of? What happened that might have set their life off on this destructive path?

By invoking curiosity, you at least challenge yourself to step out of judgment and open your heart and mind to their experience, which likely includes deep pain and suffering.

This doesn't mean you excuse their behavior. It doesn't mean you concede. It doesn't mean you need to be soft. It simply means you approach that person with a little more humanity while standing up for what is important to you.

You can still make tough decisions and maintain strong boundaries while holding an underlying premise of compassion. If not compassion, then curiosity. If not curiosity, at least common humanity.

The Divisiveness of Judgment

Judgment abounds during divorce: judgment of your former partner and judgment of yourself; judgment from other people and judgment from within; judgment of your behaviors, judgment of your path, and judgment of your decisions.

Especially common is for you and your former partner to feel a strong sense of being pitted against each other, feeling like it's "you versus me" or "us versus them." Your former partner is now your rival. You no longer understand or agree with their opinions, their behaviors, their choices, or the way they react to things. You feel they are unfair, unreasonable, selfish, and out to get you. You feel certain you wouldn't have reacted in the same way, had you been in their shoes.

Whereas once you considered yourselves fairly similar—having compatible beliefs, behaviors, and approaches to life—you now feel quite dissimilar, like you belong to different categories of people.

- ◆ I am loyal; you are a cheater.
- ◆ I am reasonable; you are selfish.
- ◆ I am doing everything I can to keep the peace. You are constantly waging war between us.
- ◆ I am levelheaded; you are rash.
- ◆ I am a good parent; you are not.

...and the list goes on.

This mental classification and divisiveness actually triggers physiological responses in your brain that inhibit you from interacting with your partner in a healthy, productive manner. Before, when you perceived your partner as similar to you or "on the same team," your brain classified them as part of your in-group.

When someone in your in-group experiences pain, your mirror neurons fire up and activate the same neural circuitry that activates when *you* are the one in pain.[7] To your brain, it doesn't make much difference if you are actually *experiencing* the pain or if you are *watching* someone in your in-group experience pain—the same neural regions activate. You empathize with their pain and are inclined to connect, align, help, and support that person.

During divorce, you now find yourself at odds with your former partner: You judge their character and see yourselves as dissimilar. Your brain begins to classify them as being part of your out-group. *Now* when you see them in pain, your mirror neurons become much less activated, as does the associated pain matrix in your brain. You literally *don't feel their pain* whereas before, you did. When someone shifts to being part of your out-group, you lose a large part of your capacity to empathize with them: You feel distant, removed, and almost numb to their struggle. A fascinating look into one such study can be seen in the PBS series *The Brain*, which is also accessible as a short YouTube video.[8]

There are many studies that have researched how our brains respond differently to people we consider to be in our in-group versus our out-group. These studies have looked at various in-group and out-group classifications, including race, political party, religious affiliation, and even sports teams. Regardless of the association, the results are consistent: Humans' innate response to seeing people in pain is, "I feel what you feel *if you are similar to me*."[9] This not only affects how we *feel* about the other person, but also how we *behave* toward them: People are more inclined to actually lend a hand when someone in their in-group needs assistance, but not when someone in their out-group is in need.[10] Further, when we believe we've been treated unfairly by someone in our out-group, we have an increased desired for revenge, but not if the perpetrator was part of our in-group.[11]

Thus, when you begin considering your spouse as more dissimilar than similar to you, they become part of your out-group. This can quickly erode the possibility of finding alignment, respect, and compromise. Rather, you are now more likely to feel apathy, separation, and desire for revenge. This subconscious response may have contributed to the downfall of your marriage if it happened long before the divorce; it is also likely acting as an impediment to moving forward together post-separation.

Shifted Perceptions Often Precipitate Divorce

Subconsciously demoting your partner to your out-group is just one change that can happen both before and during divorce. By learning about some of these common subconscious shifts in thoughts and behavior, you might begin to recognize that your tainted view of your partner is not so much a reflection of his or her diminished character, but rather a reflection of the unhealthy relationship tendencies that were present between you. As you read through the following generalization of a typical relationship's path to divorce, consider which patterns might have been present in your relationship.

- In the early years of partnership, you see your partner as part of your in-group: They are "like you." You feel a sense of camaraderie and empathy toward them. In general, you feel positive about your partner and your relationship together.

- As your relationship progresses, you become more and more confident that your partnership is stable. As such, your brain assumes that it no longer needs to make a conscious effort to procure and secure the relationship. Since the conscious brain only has the capacity to govern approximately 5 percent of your daily behaviors, it needs to be picky about what it spends its limited resources on: When something becomes stable (like your relationship), the conscious brain passes that secured item to the subconscious brain to manage in order to allocate its precious resources to the aspects of life that need more immediate attention (such as advancing your career, raising your children, paying the bills, and planning your next vacation). The subconscious brain then picks up the slack and powerfully manages the remaining 95 percent of your daily behaviors: things like muscle movement, cooking, driving, eating, showering...and, eventually, your interactions with your partner. Unfortunately, when your subconscious mind begins to govern these interactions, your dynamics shift: Whereas initially you were interacting together from your respective *conscious* brains, paying keen attention to your intentions of how you *wanted* to behave, now you are interacting with each other from your respective *subconscious* brains, each reverting back to the learned behaviors, old habits, and preconditioned responses that you learned throughout life, but were hoping to change. Not only do you shift from conscious brain interactions to subconscious brain interactions, but since the subconscious brain is a whopping 1 million times faster than the conscious brain, it picks up on more of the nuances, behaviors, reactions, and annoyances from your partner than your conscious brain did!* Therefore, as your interactions together are governed more and more by your subconscious minds, your unhelpful behaviors and reactions are becoming more prevalent and you start to become more annoyed with each other.[12]

♦ As the disconnect widens, you begin interpreting things in a more negative light (negative sentiment override) and fear that you might be headed toward divorce. In an effort to stay alert to threats, your brain becomes ultra-aware of the moments and behaviors that support your suspicion that your relationship might be failing (cognitive bias). With these potential threats seeming more and more prevalent and realistic, the fear of losing your relationship gets magnified and your alarm system activates, sending you into amygdala hijack. Your rational thinking becomes overpowered by your emotional responses—especially during arguments and triggering moments—and the situation deteriorates even more.

---

*The subconscious brain can process 40 million nerve impulses per second, whereas the conscious brain can only process 40 nerve impulses per second.

◆ By the time you are in the midst of (or post-) divorce, you typically see your partner as having qualities that are quite different from you; you consider them now as part of your out-group. You feel more judgmental and less empathetic toward them. You may even want revenge if you feel you've been treated unfairly. This creates hostile energy between you, which makes it difficult to move forward together productively and detracts from your own ability to cultivate a peaceful heart in the midst of this traumatic experience.

◆ You want to heal and find that sense of inner peace in spite of this experience, but you're not sure how. It sometimes doesn't even seem possible, given how stubborn and unreasonable your former partner is being.

Which parts can you identify with? Understanding the patterns and tendencies that you have likely been up against is the first step in initiating change; with heightened awareness comes the power to change the mental framework and habits that are not serving you well.

Awareness is the first step in empowering change.

Let's see how brain training can help you break some of these limiting mental frameworks and cultivate a more peaceful heart during divorce.

What Is Brain Training?

One of the most powerful ways to train your brain is through meditation. Perhaps you are skeptical about meditation or have preconceived notions about it, but meditation is actually a pragmatic approach to increasing the efficiency of your brain and your subconscious responses. For thousands of years, many cultures have known about the effectiveness of meditation. Now science is catching up and we are finally able to measure the effects and benefits of meditation on our brains through the use of functional magnetic resonance imaging (fMRI). Let's look in a little more depth at what meditation is and what it can do for us.

Wikipedia describes meditation as, "a practice where an individual uses a technique—such as mindfulness, or focusing the mind on a particular object, thought, or activity—to train attention and awareness, and achieve a mentally clear and emotionally calm and stable state."

Traditional definitions for meditation are closely aligned with this definition as well:

- The Tibetan word is *gom*, which means to "familiarize or to habituate."
- In Pali (the 2,600-year-old language of the Buddhist texts), the word is *bhavana*, which means "to cultivate," as in planting crops.

There are many types of meditation, each serving a different purpose in the type of brain training they provide. Some meditations train your brain to be more focused; others, to be more aware of what's going on around you. Some to calm the mind, some to calm the body. Some to decrease stress, some to increase emotional awareness. It's like physical exercise: You train differently according to the results you hope to achieve. A swimmer, a body builder, and a basketball player will all train in different ways, according to what muscles and reflexes they are looking to strengthen.[13]

One type of meditation that can have profound effects on your ability to cultivate a peaceful heart during divorce is mindfulness meditation. As reported by Harvard Health, mindfulness meditation is increasingly integrated into healthcare settings and solutions because there is evidence it improves emotional and physical health in a myriad of ways including improved cell health and reduced anxiety, stress, depression, chronic pain, psoriasis, headache, high blood pressure, and high cholesterol.[14]

Research is still relatively new, but the trend in studies also consistently shows benefits ranging from more fulfilling interpersonal relationships and increased happiness levels to enhanced brain function. A study from the University of Massachusetts Medical School's Center for Mindfulness, for example, found that after eight weeks in a mindfulness-based stress reduction (MBSR) program, meditators showed an increase in gray matter in the hippocampus (which heavily influences learning, memory, and regulation of emotions), as well as regions associated with recalling the past, imagining the future, empathy, introspection, and the ability to acknowledge the viewpoint of others. In addition, the meditators showed a decrease in gray matter in the amygdala, which is the region associated with fear, anxiety, and stress.[15]

As we saw earlier, there are both dedicated and integrated practices of meditation. We will continue to explore both with specific exercises designed toward retraining your brain and shifting how you think about yourself, your former spouse, and your relationship. This will help heal your heart, ease your pain, and set the foundation for a healthier path forward.

Training Your Brain to Promote Healing

Let's start by recalling that humans have a natural tendency to simplify: labeling people and situations into black-and-white, either/or, in-group/out-group, and other all-or-nothing categories. We choose to give up accuracy in favor of simplicity and this distorts our perception of reality. The more often we think about something with our imposed categorization, the more deeply entrenched that association becomes in our brain.

For example, perhaps when you think about your former partner, you have thoughts about how selfish and self-serving they are. This forms a neural pathway between "partner" and "selfish." The more often you think about your partner being selfish, the more established that pathway becomes. Eventually, it creates a superhighway in your brain. Now whenever you think about your partner, the brain signals take the path of least resistance, traveling down that superhighway and ending up at "selfish" by default. This is neuroplasticity: the brain's ability to reorganize itself and form new neural connections. We can take advantage of the brain's neuroplasticity by understanding that "neurons that fire together wire together."

If you no longer want certain pathways to be present (like "ex-wife" and "selfish"), you can intentionally train your brain to create and strengthen alternative pathways. Over time, after repeating these exercises and strengthening these new connections, your brain will switch its default association to another thought; perhaps "ex-wife" will now lead to "doing her best," "protecting herself," or "scared for her future." These superhighways will become the new default and your automatic response toward her will be more helpful, both when you think about her and when you interact with her.

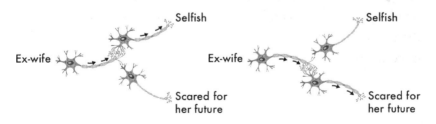

Neurons that fire together wire together

Here are two types of meditations that can help train your brain to respond more productively to your former partner: Just Like Me and Lovingkindness. Just Like Me will help you see your former partner as part of your in-group (and, thus, increase your capacity for empathy and productive interactions with them, and decrease the desire for revenge), and Lovingkindness will help to reduce contention by genuinely wishing them well.

Again, this does not mean you will necessarily let your guard down, concede points that are important to you, or succumb to their emotional pressure. It will, however, help you to approach your partner in a more humane, neutral, and loving way without giving up your boundaries.

These two meditations are very effective when practiced together and can be done in either a dedicated setting (like sitting down for five or ten minutes and focusing solely on these exercises) or in a more integrated fashion (in the moment and sprinkled throughout your day). They can also be practiced with other people you encounter throughout your day, such as the grocery store clerk you hardly notice as you rush through the checkout, that quirky colleague down the hall that you have trouble relating to, or even a political figure who riles you up on a nightly basis.

Below are sample scripts for both the dedicated and integrated practices of these meditations; feel free to customize them and make them your own. As you read through them now, practice applying them to your former partner. If you have a photo of them handy, pull that out and look at their image while you go through the meditation. If you don't have a picture, simply recall their face in your mind.

Just Like Me and Lovingkindness (Dedicated Practice)

Begin by closing or lowering your eyes and inviting your mind to calm down: Let the hustle and bustle of the day fade to the background and the chaos in your mind settle like the snow in a snow globe. Take a few deep breaths to allow this to happen.

Pay attention to your breath. What does it feel like to breathe in and out? Pretend like you're experiencing breathing for the first time—watch what it's like with the utmost fascination. Spend a few moments here, noticing.

When thoughts come into your mind, that's okay—just note that they're there and gently let them float away, bringing your attention back to your breath.

Once your heart, mind, and body feel settled, think about your former partner. Look at a picture of them or recall them in your mind. Become aware that he or she is a human being, just like you. Take a few breaths while you look at their picture and let that awareness sink in—he or she is a human being, just like you.

Then, while still looking at the photo or recalling their face, slowly read through the phrases below, pausing after each:

> *This person has a body and a mind, just like me.*
>
> *This person has thoughts and feelings, just like me.*
>
> *This person has experienced physical and emotional pain and suffering, just like me.*
>
> *This person has at some time been sad, disappointed, angry, or hurt, just like me.*

This person has felt unworthy or inadequate, just like me.

This person worries and is frightened sometimes, just like me.

This person will die someday, just like me.

This person is learning about life, just like me.

This person is probably struggling, just like me.

This person wishes to be free from pain and suffering, just like me.

This person wishes to be safe and healthy, just like me.

This person wishes to be happy, just like me.

This person wishes to be loved, just like me.

Now, allow wishes for well-being to arise:

May you be well.

May you be free from pain and suffering.

May you be at ease.

May you be loved.

May your heart be at peace.

…because you are a fellow human being, just like me.

Bring your attention back to your breath and spend a few moments being in the peaceful spaciousness, your heart-space open.

Just Like Me and Lovingkindness (Integrated Practice)

In any given moment, and especially just before—or during—an interaction with your partner, look at their face or recall them in your mind. Then, bring to mind a simplified version of the above;

it does not need to be the same every time. Simply acknowledge some aspect of your shared humanity and wish them well. Perhaps something like the following:

> *This person wants to be happy, healthy, and loved, just like me.*
> *May your heart be at peace.*

Or

> *This person wants to be free of pain and suffering, just like me.*
> *May you live a life of ease.*

The beauty of these practices is that you can do them completely independently of your partner—they don't have to do a thing and yet, it will still improve your interactions. By simply shifting how you think about them, you give yourselves better chances for success, healing, and forward motion. Perhaps this will lead to compromise and a common understanding, or maybe it won't. At the very least, you avoid exacerbating the downward spiral by decreasing the amount of animosity and aggression you feel.

> *"Realizing that the other person is also just like me is the basis on which we can develop compassion, not only toward those around us but also toward our enemy. Normally, when we think about our enemy, we think about harming him. Instead, try to remember that the enemy is also a human being, just like you."*
> —His Holiness the Fourteenth Dalai Lama

Consistently pay attention to the thoughts you are having about your former partner and begin training your brain to see them as a human being, just like you—someone who wants to be happy, healthy, and loved. It might not change what you are asking for or what gets decided upon, but it will change the quality of your interactions and promote healing, both for you and for the relationship.

Bridge the Divide through Recognizing Your Common Humanity

As you watch your former partner react in ways you think are uncalled for or off base, soften your judgment of them by seeing the humanity of this person in front of you.

Your partner does not *want* to be in so much pain. If they knew a way around it, they would take it. You may not understand or agree with why they're acting a certain way, but you can still choose to be compassionate.

Choosing compassion will foster open-heartedness for your soul, whereas judgment will foster closed-heartedness.

Release your partner from blame. They are human, doing their best in the current set of circumstances, just as *you* are human, doing *your* best in the current set of circumstances. Just because you are experiencing it differently than they are, is no reason to judge. You cannot know exactly what they are thinking or feeling, or what is influencing them in any given interaction; their circumstances are not your own.

When entering into discussions or going through mediation or divorce, try to approach your former partner with an underlying premise of compassion. Remember that he or she is going through a tumultuous process, just like you. Their identity is also crumbling and will need rebuilding. Their dreams are also being shattered. Regardless of who you think was at fault for creating this situation, neither of you envisioned it would happen to you and yet here you find yourselves.

If you can, remind yourself of who this person was when you first entered into relationship with them. What were their hopes and dreams? What attracted you to them? What was it about them that you wanted to be around for the rest of your life?

Try to see these qualities in your partner, even now. In doing so, you are not minimizing the struggles or abuse that may have arisen in the meantime, but you are broadening your perspective and softening your view of them.

What are the ways in which they might be hurting?

Remember, unless it was an arranged marriage or a marriage forced upon you, you chose this person as your partner. If you have children together, he or she is still your children's parent.

Regardless, they deserve your support and well-wishes for a life of ease if for no other reason than that they are a human being, just like you. Despite your pain, differences, and anger, you can still wish for them a happy, fulfilling life.

PRINCIPLE 3

MAKE SELF-RESPECT
A PRIORITY

 CAPTAIN'S LOG

"The fact that I am compassionate toward you does not mean I am weak. I will stand up for my self-respect. I feel for you, yet I will not engage with you when you are doing or saying things I feel are degrading to me. I can be compassionate *and* stand up for myself. These healthy boundaries will ultimately serve us both better." —S.M.

Having compassion toward your former partner does not mean you coddle them, condone their behavior, or submit to their every wish or need.

More often than not, there is a fair amount of emotional artillery that is being fired at you from your soon-to-be ex. It's like your ship is under siege by a barrage of cannon fire as your ex-spouse tries over and over to blast holes in the very essence of your being. All their hate, anger, hurt, and frustration comes firing away from across the emotional abyss; they are ultimately hoping to bring you down with them, as they are drowned by pain and agony. Somehow it seems (falsely) that the more they attack, the more it lessens their pain, makes them right, and reinforces the idea that divorce is indeed the right path forward. Of course, we cannot know their intentions, but this is often how it *feels* during divorce and your partner may feel this coming from you as well, regardless of whether you intend it or not.

Not only is the barrage probably coming from your former spouse, but it might also be coming from within yourself (and perhaps people around you, too). You have judgments, questions, doubts, and insecurities about who you are, how you are handling it, how you contributed, what you can do about it, and how you're ever going to get through it without being brutally ripped down and stripped in the process.

In the midst of this landscape, preserving self-respect is critical.

Do Not Allow Abuse to Continue

During times of divorce, your partner (like you) may feel like their life is spinning out of control—they can't control the outcome of the divorce, the support payments, your actions, or how the kids are raised at your house. There is so much that is out of their control. When feeling powerless like this, your partner (or you) may grasp for control wherever it might be found.

"Domestic violence and abuse stem from a desire to
gain and maintain power and control
over an intimate partner."[16]

If you are being spoken to harshly or treated in a way that does not feel fair or right to you, stop the interaction immediately and safely remove yourself from the situation if you can. Do not allow it to continue. The more you allow it, the further the line of permission gets pushed. Especially in the case of abuse, keep in mind the adage:

Don't ask why someone keeps hurting you—
ask why you keep letting them.

There are a myriad of resources available if you feel like you might be the victim of abuse. Abuse is sometimes blatant and obvious like financial bullying, physical or sexual abuse, or verbal threats to physically harm you. It can also be more subtle—so subtle that sometimes the victim doesn't even realize they're being abused.

In these more subtle cases, the interpersonal dynamics have gradually shifted from neutral interactions to more abusive behavior. Since there have been no incidents that are notably different than the ones before, it is often hard to recognize when the line of acceptability gets crossed. The victim has become so used to being gradually treated with more and more disrespect that they often don't realize how far away from neutral it has become until something becomes so blatant that they wake up and look astonishedly at the dynamics that have been present.

You Are Establishing Norms for This New Phase of Relationship

Regardless of whether abuse is present, you are likely relating to each other in a different way now than you used to. Your relationship, as you knew it, is over. Even if you remain connected through children or other shared responsibilities, the previous relationship is finished and a new one is being established. During this time, it is crucial that you do what you can to instill positive behaviors, strong boundaries, and healthy ways of behaving together that will ultimately serve you both as you step into this new future together. Take the lead to redefine your dynamics: Insist on holding clear boundaries and do what you need to do to preserve your safety and self-respect.

Understanding Healthy Boundaries

Boundaries are especially important when one partner is aggressive and the other is more of a peacemaker. This may have been your traditional dynamic during the marriage or it could be a new dynamic that is surfacing during divorce, perhaps due to one person feeling betrayed, hurt, or taken advantage of and the other person feeling remorseful or guilty about things they have done to contribute to the relationship's demise. In this dynamic, when one person is compassionate and understanding and the other is out for revenge, it is extremely important for the compassionate partner to maintain strong boundaries.

The purpose of boundaries is not to try to control the other person or coerce them into doing something you want them to do. Rather, it is to tell someone, "This is the space that I need for my well-being; if you disregard that, here are the consequences. I will follow through with these consequences because I care about protecting my well-being."

You can think of relational boundaries like property boundaries: You put a fence around your property as a demarcation, meaning that when somebody crosses the line, they know they are in your space and that this space is under your management. If someone crosses that boundary uninvited, there are logical consequences; if someone is invited in but then misbehaves or disrespects you or your property, there are also logical consequences. It's like a No Trespassing sign: If someone chooses to cross it despite the warning, it is their choice to do so, knowing full well what the consequences are. When you enforce them, it's not because you are trying to hurt them or inflict pain; you are simply protecting your space and well-being.

In relationships, it is important to understand the differences between "boundaries without consequences," "boundaries with consequences," and "threats." There are subtle differences, but they are important ones.

Boundaries without Consequences	Boundaries with Consequences	Threats
"You need to have the kids back to me by 5 PM."	"You need to have the kids back to me by 5 PM. If you don't, I'm going to subtract that time from your next visit and bring the kids late. I'm also going to add it to the log of instances where you have not respected our agreed-upon time for exchanges."	"You need to have the kids back to me by 5 PM or I won't let you see them next time."
"Let me know by 12 PM tomorrow whether you agree to extend my vacation with the kids by two days."	"Let me know by 12 PM tomorrow whether you agree to extend my vacation with the kids by two days. If I don't hear from you, I'll assume you agree to the extension."	"Let me know by 12 PM tomorrow whether you agree to extend my vacation with the kids by two days. If you don't tell me by then, I'm going to take them anyway and I'll be sure to say no next time you ask me for something."
"Don't yell at me."	"Don't yell at me. If you do, I'm walking out."	"Don't yell at me. If you do, I'm going to record it and post it on Facebook to prove to people how you've been abusing me."

(Boundaries without Consequences)	(Boundaries with Consequences)	(Threats)
"You're too angry and I don't want to be around you like that. Go spend the night at a hotel."	"You're too angry and I don't want to be around you like that. Go spend the night at a hotel or I'm taking the kids to my parents' house for the weekend."	"You're too angry and I don't want to be around you like that. Go spend the night at a hotel or I'll kick you out of the house for good."
Boundaries without consequences provide no reason for the other person to change their behavior. They are empty requests and you become disempowered.	Boundaries with consequences make it clear that if certain expectations are not upheld, there will be a specific action that follows. This action is logical, timely, and is meant to protect your well-being, not inflict injury on the other person.	Threats are usually made in anger and are trying to scare someone into behaving a particular way or else they'll be injured physically, financially, relationally, or otherwise.

To further clarify the nuances between "boundaries with consequences" and "threats," consider the following:

Boundaries with Consequences	Threats
Made when you are calm and levelheaded.	Made in anger, usually in the middle of an argument.
Gives the message: "If you do this, I will protect myself and those under my charge."	Gives the message: "If you do this, I will punish you or hurt you."
Meant to let the other person know what logical action will come next if they do not change their behavior.	Meant to scare the other person so much that they change their behavior out of fear.
The pain incurred encourages growth and appropriate behavior change.	The pain incurred causes further injury, not growth.
The intention is to steer your relationship toward more healthy interactions and establish expectations and norms.	The intention is to get even by hurting the other person as much as they've hurt you.

You can absolutely have strong boundaries and still be compassionate, because boundaries with consequences are not meant to hurt the other person; they are meant to inspire healthy change and protect your own well-being. It is possible to protect your own well-being while still being compassionate.

On the other hand, if you are compassionate and *do not* insist on boundaries with consequences (meaning you either have weak boundaries or boundaries without consequences), you will likely get walked all over, particularly if your former partner is coming from a place of more aggressive energy, righteousness, or lack of desire to understand or co-parent productively together.

Remember, you don't put up a fence to try to control others' behaviors when they're outside your property; you put it up to protect your space and make it clear that when someone enters, there are logical, appropriate consequences. The severity of the consequence will depend on the severity of the infraction. As long as you're not making the consequence out of anger and with the desire to inflict pain or punishment, it's probably a boundary with a consequence. You are not making the other person do something; it's their choice whether to cross that line or not. If they choose to cross the line, they do so consciously—with full knowledge of what will happen next.

Assertive Is Not Aggressive

It is also crucial that you learn to assert yourself in a way that is not aggressive but is standing firm in your beliefs and values while trying to find middle ground where possible.

Assertiveness can easily be misinterpreted as aggression, particularly if your partner is used to you being more passive or accommodating. Many times, people who tend to be peacemakers have a hard time standing up for their boundaries for fear of creating conflict or appearing aggressive or harsh. Standing up for your needs and self-respect is not aggressive, it is assertive—and assertive is healthy.

When I was working with my coach during my divorce, I came up with a metaphor that beautifully illustrated the distinction between assertion and aggression, and the reason why assertiveness is often misinterpreted as aggression:

Imagine you are standing inside of a giant balloon—one that surrounds you completely, one or two feet from your body. This balloon is your homeostasis, your neutral state. When your partner pushes into your balloon from the outside and you do not push back, your balloon will naturally expand outward in another region. If you are a peacemaker, you are probably used to allowing your partner to push into your balloon—to push into your homeostasis. It seems harmless because your balloon just expands in another area. However, your passive response means your balloon is repeatedly stretching to accommodate the intrusion. Over time, it will inevitably become weaker and may even become so thin that it eventually pops.

In order to preserve the cellular structure and strength of your metaphorical balloon during divorce (in other words, to hold your ground, protect your homeostasis, and maintain your self-respect), it is important that you not remain passive: When your partner pushes their hand against your balloon (disturbing your homeostasis), metaphorically reach out with your hand and push their hand back out to neutral. This is assertiveness; this is protecting your homeostasis; this is looking out for your overall well-being and continued strength. Your partner, however, may not be used to you pushing against their hand—they're used to being able to push against you without you putting counterpressure on their hand. Now that you are pushing their hand back to neutral, they feel an opposing force where they are used to feeling little or none. This force is what they interpret as aggression because it has a lot of the same physical energy— you are pushing against them. It isn't actually aggression though unless you push past your balloon's neutral state into *their* homeostasis, and do so with an intent to punish or harm.

This difference in the intentionality of your pushback is important: If you are looking to protect yourself, your children, or your well-being—and are attempting to do that while maintaining respect for the other person and without intent to punish or harm them—it is likely assertiveness. If you are pushing back in order to cause pain, seek retribution, inflict punishment, or otherwise injure or attack your former partner, it is more likely aggression (which is not healthy).

Along with aggression often comes anger, and anger is often misunderstood. You may think anger is unhealthy (and especially counterproductive when trying to cultivate a peaceful heart!), and it is if you react to it unconsciously, let it fester, or let it rashly dictate your words, behavior, and emotions.

Anger in and of itself, though, can be healthy. It's there for a reason: It's usually a sign that something you care about is not being honored. Maybe you are not being treated with respect, maybe there is an injustice that needs righting, or maybe you are angry with *yourself* for not holding stronger boundaries. Whatever the case may be, if you look beneath anger, there's usually a person or value that needs to be stood up for and honored more. Anger is, therefore, useful in bringing our attention to something that needs to be defended; we just need to learn how to respond to the anger consciously and productively, managing it appropriately so it doesn't fester or cause further wounding.

Standing up for your values and being assertive might feel scary. You may feel resistance, either from within yourself or from your partner. You may feel uncomfortable. You may not want to even acknowledge the anger. Due to this discomfort, it can be tempting to concede, appeasing the other person in order to calm their anger and keep the peace in the moment. But oftentimes, this newly acquired peace is only temporary. It relieves the pressure in the moment but can actually fuel problems and frustration in the long term because you are not insisting on healthy dynamics up front.

Being assertive is one way to address these important points head-on so they don't linger and cause ongoing resentment. Remember, you are establishing guidelines for your future dynamics together in this new iteration of your relationship. You want it to be governed by clarity, fairness, confidence, and well-defined boundaries. Though it may be uncomfortable, it will set a precedence for more positive interactions together and will ultimately serve you both better.

Let's apply this to co-parenting after divorce: Let's suppose you don't believe it's in your children's best interest to live with their other parent (perhaps there are other physical or emotional dangers present like abuse or neglect). It is important that you state this, either directly to the co-parent or to a judge or mediator. Imagine you say: "The kids should not live with their mom because she neglects them." Now, envision the impact if you shared this from 1) a place of compassion and humanity (while still holding clarity and conviction) or 2) from a place of retribution, anger, hostility, and fear. The *feeling* behind those two ways of communicating is enormously different and, as such, the impact is enormously different as well. Not only are you much more likely to pave the way for productive conversation with the former approach, but you are also more likely to be seen as reasonable, sensible, and trustworthy by third parties such as the judge, mediator, or recommending counselor.

Using Code Words

If you find that your interactions spiral quickly out of control and that it's difficult to maintain composure or make progress without getting into an argument, consider establishing code words between the two of you.

These code words are agreed upon up front and carry with them certain rules and expectations: When one person says the code word, the other then knows exactly what is expected in that moment. Here are two suggested code words that can be extremely effective if both partners agree to respect their use. Of course, the actual words don't matter. Use words that make sense for the two of you; it's the context and rules behind them that are important to agree upon and uphold.

"Shield" means:
"I am feeling attacked. The statement needs to be rephrased in a less aggressive way before I am expected to respond."

Notice that there is no accusation of who is to blame and there is no assumption of who is right or wrong. All that is being said is that one person *feels* attacked—it does not mean they actually were.

By saying "shield," one person is able to let the other know (in a relatively safe and straightforward way) that they're feeling attacked; they are instinctively wanting to go into fight-or-flight mode. If fight-or-flight were to take over, it would either heighten the aggression or stop the conversation altogether as a result of their fleeing and disengaging from it. By saying "shield," this person is taking personal responsibility for the quality of their shared interaction by allowing the pair the opportunity to redirect the course of the conversation before it gets too far off the rails. It's a great way to strengthen personal boundaries of self-respect in a non-accusatory way without spiraling into the blame game, needing to go into explanations, or feeling like they're being walked all over. By simply saying "shield," there is an immediate shared understanding of what is happening and what needs to happen next.

It is also beneficial for the other person because they are able to gain an understanding of what triggers their former partner (regardless of whether they feel it is merited or not) and they are given a chance to rescind or reframe their statement in a way that helps the partnership move forward in conversation. With each occurrence, they have an opportunity to learn from the situation and be more careful about how they are speaking in the future.

Again, this does not mean one person is right and the other is wrong in their interpretation of what's happening. The person who called "shield" may be completely overreacting, or they may be completely justified. It actually doesn't matter. What matters is that the partners are both becoming more aware of what statements, tones, or attitudes are triggers, and that they are given a chance to try again without the conversation escalating or shutting down.

Little by little, as each partner becomes more aware of their partner's triggers, they learn about how they impact the other person (whether intentional or unintentional, whether reasonable or not), and they have the opportunity to learn more effective ways to communicate together.

The second code word is "bunker."

"Bunker" means:
"I am feeling too attacked. I need time to cool off before we move forward with this conversation. I will reinitiate the conversation with you within the next 24 hours."

It is critical that the person who called "bunker" must uphold their end of the bargain and reinitiate the conversation within the 24-hour period. Likewise, it is critical that the other person does not try to reinitiate the conversation during this time; they must respect the space that was requested.

As with "shield," "bunker" does not place blame. It does not assume someone is being intentionally malicious and it does not assume one person is in the right and the other is in the wrong. It is simply a means of communicating that the dynamics have degraded and one partner needs space before being expected to continue in a productive way.

There is actually a physiological reason for this. Relationship expert Dr. John Gottman runs a research center called the Love Lab, where he has analyzed the relationship dynamics of over 3,000 couples. While in the Love Lab, couples engage in normal interactions and are also asked to talk about issues that typically spawn arguments between them. The couple is video recorded and hooked up to biometric sensors while they talk about these tension-inducing topics. In essence, Dr. Gottman and his team are able to collect and analyze audio, visual, and biometric data from the couples and track these couples over time. Due to the mass of data they have collected since 1986, they are now able to predict if and when couples will divorce, based on certain observed behaviors. Gottman's findings are so accurate that in his 1992 study, he successfully predicted with 93.6 percent accuracy which couples would end up divorcing.[17] Further, his team found that couples for whom the Four Horsemen were present (criticism, contempt, defensiveness, and stonewalling) divorced after an average of 5.6 years, while emotionally disengaged couples divorced after an average of 16.2 years of marriage.[18]

When couples get into a heated debate or argument, their limbic systems activate—setting off the fight-or-flight response. Their bodies are then flooded with cortisol and adrenaline and their brains experience amygdala hijack. As you have seen on page 69, rational thinking and productive conversation is nearly impossible in this state. Dr. Gottman explains this reaction using the term "flooded," meaning that a person gets so inundated with these stress hormones that they are no longer able to effectively communicate with the other person.

In these times, calling "bunker" is effective. Taking a time-out allows the limbic system to calm down and the executive functioning centers of the brain to come back online. It is, indeed, in the best interest of both people to take a break and come back to the conversation later. It prevents the conversation from spiraling out of control in an exchange flooded with emotion and unclear thinking.

Having these code words is extremely helpful in establishing a common set of rules and expectations so that both people can learn how to communicate effectively with each other. You can start using these regardless of where you are in the divorce process. If you are in the stages of pre-divorce, they are just as helpful as if you have been divorced for 10 years but are still struggling to communicate effectively together. After using these words for some time, you will both become more attuned to what triggers the unhealthy dynamics and, as such, you will likely need to use these words less and less.

Honor Your Truth and Stay In Inner Alignment

When you think, act, or behave in ways that are not aligned with what is right and true for you, you feel a sense of internal friction and dissonance within yourself. This creates a state of "dis-ease." You are thinking and acting in ways that do not sit well with you—ways that you feel are counter to who you are as a person.

This "dis-ease" is not comfortable and, in fact, can perpetuate actual disease in the cells of your body. Sometimes this disease is explicit and tangible like cancer or chronic fatigue; sometimes it is more subtle, perhaps caused by sustained, elevated cortisol levels brought on by perpetual stress; and sometimes the dis-ease can manifest as depression or withdrawal from friends and loved ones. Regardless of the manifestation, internal dis-ease creates an unhealthy environment for your cells, your brain, your heart, and your healing.

The more you can inwardly reflect and live in alignment with your truth, the more internal ease you will create for yourself.

---

*Honoring your truth creates the space in which
a peaceful heart can emerge.*

This can manifest as reclaiming who you are as an individual, getting clear about your priorities and values, standing up for your boundaries, and forging your own path in life instead of listening to what others say you "should" be doing.

I had a particularly vivid experience of this sense of internal ease versus dis-ease about nine months after my husband and I separated. We were meeting together with a tax consultant to determine how to file our taxes for the year we separated. As we sat in her office reviewing our respective finances, the disparities between us became more and more evident:

- I was trying to enter the workforce after being a stay-at-home mom; he was enjoying a steady, dependable job.

- I was starting my own business, wasn't quite sure how to market it and make it profitable, and was constantly re-evaluating whether I was on the right track; he enjoyed his work, was well respected in the company, and was in his 14th year with them.

- I was barely breaking even in my business; he was making a sizable salary and had great benefits.

- I was house-sitting in someone else's home to save money; he was in our lovely, large family home.

I felt repeatedly humiliated throughout our appointment. My self-worth was on the verge of collapse and I was actively holding back tears the entire hour. I felt worthlessness. Crushed.

When the appointment ended, I hightailed it out of the office and burst out crying when I closed my car door.

A few minutes into the drive, I took several deep breaths to try to calm myself down. I acknowledged how overwhelmed and worthless I was feeling and how embarrassing that appointment was: All the disparities that had arisen were true!

Then I recognized the story I was telling myself: that these differences were proof that I was not successful, that I was doing things wrong, and that the disparity was a reflection of our relative worth. *This was the story of my perceiving eye. It was just that: a story!*

Then I backed up and reoriented toward my observing eye. I realized that these disparities were, in fact, true, but I was also very much in inner alignment with what mattered to me:

- I was choosing to start my own business so that I could do what I love, make an impact in the world, have the flexibility to be home with my children after school, and have a better career trajectory than I otherwise would have had.

- It is normal to have a negative balance or be just breaking even in your business in the first year.

- I consciously chose to house-sit because it allowed me the financial flexibility to start my own business and be at home with the kids, even if I wasn't making much money to begin with.

- It was one of my highest priorities to be at home with my young children as we went through the divorce so that they would be nurtured and cared for as they also went through the transition. Additionally, I didn't want to add to their trauma by immediately going from having a stay-at-home mom to having a full-time, work-in-the-office mom.

In a few deep breaths, and with the recognition that my interpreting eye had been believing a story that actually wasn't true for me, my whole persona changed. I instantly felt a weight lifted off me. My sense of inner peace and confidence returned.

This is the type of dramatic internal shift you, too, can have when you practice these principles.

The more aligned you are with your higher self, the less it matters what other people think of you or what they choose to do. You know who you are, what you represent, and how you are engaging with the world. Coming from this place of inner grounding and confidence can help promote a more stable journey through this tumultuous time.

Find Strength Wherever You Can

In the midst of such upheaval, it can be difficult to find your footing, even with conscious intent. When your whole foundation is rocked by divorce, it can be extremely challenging to find the confidence to stand up for yourself. You may feel unworthy, low in self-respect, or even so unsure of what's reasonable that you don't know *what* you stand for anymore. You may have conflicting thoughts that make you feel unsteady and unconfident—thoughts such as:

- ◆ I care deeply about being fair, but I'm not even sure what fair is anymore.

- ◆ I want to be respectful of my former partner and I also want to stand up for my self-respect and well-being. Sometimes those don't both feel possible, particularly when it gets contentious.

- I want to be assertive for what I feel is rightfully due to me, but I don't want it to come across as uncooperative or aggressive.

- Am I giving up too much or am I not asking for enough?

- Am I nit-picking or do these things matter in the bigger scheme of things?

- I want to be heard genuinely, but I'm often misinterpreted.

- I need to share important parts of our story with the judge or mediator, but I dread bringing them up because I know my partner will probably feel attacked and I hate the thought of doing that to them.

- I expect to feel attacked as well, but I feel ill-equipped to respond because I'm not sure what my partner is preparing against me.

- I want to support my children's relationship with their co-parent, but I don't approve of the parenting at the other house. It is gut-wrenching to let the children go there without me, yet I know they need to spend time with the other parent as well.

In the midst of such confusion, find grounding, clarity, and confidence however you can. Don't be ashamed to use trinkets, symbols, mantras, hacks, or rituals that help you connect to your inner strength.

One person I knew was intensely nervous before her court appointment. She arrived at the meeting 30 minutes early, went inside the women's restroom, and went through a whole ritual of presencing exercises:

- She wore a necklace that was given to her by a friend who bequeathed it to her as a symbol of inner strength and divine protection.

- She brought a memento from her children's infant stages to keep her focused on their well-being and best interest.

- She dabbed on essential oils to promote mental clarity and invigoration.

- She sat on the toilet and read through letters that were generously and lovingly written by friends and colleagues, offering encouragement and attestation of her character and strength.

- She read through reminders she had written to herself about why she was here, what she wanted to accomplish, and how she wanted to comport herself.

- She meditated.

- She embodied a warrior stance for a few minutes in the bathroom stall: her fists on her hips, her feet spread apart, and her chest and chin held high.

In these contentious situations, verbal accusations, judgments, and character degradation happen with abandon. It's easy to start believing these and succumb to the emotional pressure put on you by your former partner. Do whatever you can to broaden your perspective, and reach out to those around you who know you, love you, and see you for who you are. Surround yourself with them, ask for notes, create symbols, gather pictures, or write a list of names of all the people who love and support you.

Any and all of these practices can help you maintain composure and strength during these rocky times. Particularly when you are feeling tossed about in the thick of the emotional turmoil or in stressful circumstances such as mediation or court, do whatever it takes for you to reconnect to your true nature—reminding yourself of who you are outside of this turmoil. Keep your intentions steady and clear.

Step Aside, Ego!

Broken relationships and strained dynamics happen to good, well-intentioned people as well as to people you might not think so highly of. When you are overwhelmed with feelings of unworthiness, guilt, failure, and hopelessness—when you feel like there must be something wrong with you because you're now a divorcee—it can be helpful to remember that divorce is not necessarily a reflection of one person or the other. There is also a third entity involved that often gets overlooked: the relationship itself.

When you are in relationship with someone, there is you, there is your partner, and there is the energy between you: the exchanges, the actions, the impacts, the misunderstandings, the communication.

When the relationship starts to sour, it is not necessarily an innate reflection on the lack of worthiness, value, competence, or dedication of either individual.

More often, it is a sign that something is askew between them—that the relationship itself needs tending to: perhaps that partners need to engage, issues need to be surfaced, boundaries need to be enforced, and needs must be expressed, or perhaps that the partners need to intentionally focus on acknowledging what's *good* about their partner instead of what's *bad*.

A relationship has a life cycle; it has a heartbeat and a pulse; it needs nurturing, tending to, and urgent care sometimes. The relationship needs to be fed, exercised, and mentored. It needs to grow and learn, just as both individuals do.

Without explicitly realizing that the relationship is its own entity, you can fall into the trap of blaming the relationship's downfall on your partner. After all, you know *you* were doing your best, so it couldn't possibly have been your fault, right? But when you recognize that the relationship is, in fact, a third entity that needs tending to, you can start to understand how both of you could be doing your best, but that the energy between you becomes malnourished or disconnected. Of course, both people are the ones who are in control over the dynamics of the relationship, so they *do* have a say in the matter. The relationship's demise, however, is not a pure reflection on either individual's efforts or innate worth.

Recognizing this can help promote self-care and healing because instead of there being something intrinsically wrong with you as a person (or with your spouse), there is rather something amiss in the way the two of you are interacting. It becomes more about the choices and behavior and less about each person's core identity or worth. Remember, people behave uncharacteristically in times of stress. The stressful context is not an excuse for impermissible action, but understanding that it may be a stress-induced reaction can help soften your initial judgments.

When you feel like your identity and self-worth is attacked, judged, or shunned, it can crush you to your core. Keep in mind:

- You can still be a good person, even if you've struggled and made bad choices.

- Your partner's aggression is not necessarily a reflection on you. It might be their way of falsely ensuring the preservation of their own ego by placing the blame on you.

- Your relationship is a separate entity, distinct from either individual. Yes, your marriage failed, but getting divorced does not mean you are a failure.

In other words, your marital problems are not a direct reflection of your worth as a person.

This separation of ego can be a crucial step in preserving your sense of self-worth and liberating your pain and anger.

PRINCIPLE 4

DO YOUR BEST AND
LET GO OF THE REST

 CAPTAIN'S LOG

"I think of our relationship like a field; and the two of us, as caretakers of that field. I am fertilizing the soil of our field and planting the seeds I hope will grow. I cannot control which seeds you choose to plant or whether you choose to throw herbicide on our field. If a barren field is all it ever becomes, so be it. I have tended the soil and planted these seeds, so perhaps— if there is minimal herbicide thrown—trust, warmth, and positive engagement might begin to take root and sprout. We may even find ourselves in a beautiful field of bounty, come spring, having diligently tended the soil during the bleak midwinter when everything seemed barren, stark, hopeless, and desolate.

I cannot control how you choose to be, but I will bring self-respect, amicability, and compassion to our relationship." —S.M.

Tending the Field

Indeed, your relationship is now like a field with an uncertain future. Will it become overgrown and strewn with weeds and invasive plants? Will it remain hopelessly barren and crusted with sunbaked mud? Will it turn into a beautiful field, ripe for harvest? Will it be rugged and scattered with occasional wildflowers?

The soil is yours to tend. You can decide to fertilize it and prepare the soil for growth or, conversely, you can decide to continuously neglect the field (or worse, to throw pesticide on the relationship, approaching your partner with animosity, aggression, and bitterness). The choice is yours to make.

The fate of the field will ultimately depend on how both of you treat the soil, but at least you can do your part in nurturing it for growth and flourishment. Despite your potential aversion to it now, will you accept the challenge? Is it worth it for the well-being of your children? Is it worth it to preserve your ongoing relationships with your partner's family? Is it worth it, if for no other reason than to promote your own healing?

Accept that divorce is now your reality and do your best to get through it with grace and ease—connecting to what is genuinely important to you, setting your sights on healthy aspirations for the two of you, and striving to build the best relationship possible in the given context. Have boundaries; be clear. Stand up for what is needed and put consequences in place—not with an air of aggression, but with a desire for growth and healthy relationships. Do your best to give your partner the benefit of the doubt and, if you have children together, strive to promote a healthy relationship between the children and their other parent.

Heal From the Inside Out

Going through divorce is like receiving a deep puncture wound to your life's path. That part of your life and your soul will never be the same again. It is inevitable that you'll come away with scars.

There are different healing options, however.

- ◆ You can do nothing different, letting your mindset and interactions continue as they are now, letting the wound fester, and inviting anger, bitterness, resentment, frustration, and victimhood. This makes for deeper, more painful scars that are harder to heal and are more susceptible to re-wounding.

- ◆ Similarly, if you ignore the depths of the issues, pain, or emotional trauma and try to cover over them without first tending to the hurt, it's like stitching the skin shut without first cleaning out the contaminants and bacteria. This will create infection in the wound and impede the healing process.

- ◆ Alternatively, you can choose to tend to this wound, healing the tissue little by little with gentle, loving care, suturing each layer of skin as you go. You are healing yourself from the inside out, slowly over time. Go to counseling, seek wise people, attend personal growth programs, create purpose in your life, meditate, pray, journal, eat a healthy diet, exercise, and surround yourself with laughter, creativity, and meaningful relationships. This is what it is to heal. Be careful not to cover over the hurt without tending to it, but *do* engage in activities like this to help promote wellness. They will nourish your soul and your sense of self, and help you heal from the inside out. Admittedly, there will be lasting visible scars, but overall, the wound will heal with much greater integrity, strength, and resilience.

The Importance of Self-Care

Part of preserving your self-respect is prioritizing self-care during divorce.

You are probably feeling stress from many different angles: perhaps needing to get a better-paying job or a job with more flexibility so you can be with the kids; perhaps feeling miserable because of how your partner is treating you, speaking to you, and speaking about you; perhaps feeling ashamed that you're in this process at all, now having become one of the dismal statistics of broken marriages; perhaps feeling regretful about moments when you were reactive and nasty, and now wish you had responded otherwise; perhaps you are feeling taken advantage of; ...and the list goes on.

All of these feelings may be coalescing into one common message: You don't deserve any more than what you have/you are not worthy/you are broken/you have failed/you deserve to be hurting.

In the midst of such messaging, you might wonder, "Who am I to deserve self-care right now?"

As we saw earlier, stress has a physiological impact on our well-being and health. Our bodies are built to receive certain amounts of the stress hormone cortisol; it is helpful in acute times of need, like when we feel threatened and need to react quickly. However, when we are under constant stress, this continual release of cortisol can mean our system is perpetually saturated with cortisol at levels that are detrimental to our health when sustained long term. Living with high stress is not only emotionally exhausting, it is also physically damaging.

Any practices of self-care that you can incorporate can be helpful, whether they are as simple as deep breathing or getting a massage, or more elaborate like studying yoga or learning a new hobby. These nourishing practices can help you regulate your cortisol levels and promote overall health and well-being.

Self-care does not always look like taking a pause in life to do something comforting, however.

Self-care also means taking the steps you need in order to build a life for yourself that you don't need to escape from.

Maybe it looks like going to night school so that you can get a better job in a few years. Granted, it is adding stress and fatigue in the short term, but you are setting yourself up for longer-term success and health, ultimately helping you *thrive* instead of just *survive*.

The Neuroscience of Memories

There is another type of self-care, and it is this type of self-care that this book principally addresses. It is sculpting our mindset (or perhaps, we should more accurately call it our "heartset"): becoming aware of—and taking conscious control over—how we think and feel about things.

To learn more about how we can use our mindset to cultivate a more peaceful heart—even while feeling pain—let's take a look at what happens in our brains when we recall memories. Divorce is a perfect time to practice this skill, because it is a time in which we are frequently recalling (and recounting) the precipitating events and current trials of our divorce; it is a time when we are frequently talking about our former spouse and the plight we are experiencing with them; there is a given set of memories that we frequently revisit and bring to the forefront.

When you have an experience in life, your brain essentially imprints that information for future recall. It's like creating a

Word document for each experience you have. Then, every time you replay the experience or talk about it, you essentially retrieve the Word document, open it, read it, edit it slightly based on your current environment or mood, and then save it again, placing it back in your brain's filing cabinet for later retrieval.

When the brain creates a memory, connections between neurons are established. These connections, or synapses, can be strengthened or weakened according to how often they are used. When we activate specific neuropathways repetitively (like recalling a memory over and over), those synaptic connections are strengthened and new synaptic connections along this neuropathway are created. The gray matter grows.

When there are neurocircuits that are not used often (like memories that we don't think about often), the synaptic connections die off, making way for new connections to be formed when needed. This allows the brain to be more efficient; it's like cleaning out its hard drive to make way for new data to be encoded.[19]

This neuroplasticity allows our brains to adjust to new situations and changes in our environment by rewiring itself and adapting its structure as we go through life.[20] Interestingly though, it is the brain's ability to adapt that also influences the accuracy of our memories.

Donna Bridge, a postdoctoral fellow at Northwestern University Feinberg School of Medicine, explains how memories are, in fact, not static images imprinted at the time of the event. Rather, every time we remember the event, our recollection becomes a little more distorted—even to the point of being totally false with each retrieval. Something as simple as our environment or the mood we are in can be unintentionally integrated into the memory when we recall it.[21] It's like superimposing two images and then saving it as one image.[22] Our memories are so susceptible to new information that even something as small as how a question is phrased can cause the memory to be altered in a different way.

For example, in a study by memory expert Elizabeth Loftus, participants were shown video footage of two cars crashing into each other. Some were then questioned, "How fast were the cars going when they hit each other?" Others were questioned, "How fast were the cars going when they smashed into each other?" The participants were then questioned one week later to see how well they recalled the event. When asked whether they had seen broken glass, most participants answered no, but those who had been asked the "smashed into" version of the question (as opposed to the "hit" version) were more likely to recall there being broken glass.[23]

Applying this to the context of divorce, if a friend asks you, "When did he start *abusing* you?" as opposed to "When did he start *mistreating* you?" you might recall the memories slightly differently. They may now be infused with more undertones of abuse than were originally present. This tendency for current information to interfere with and alter our memories is known as the misinformation effect.[24]

> *"Simply recalling a memory makes it more susceptible to being weakened, distorted, or erased."*
> —*Sam Berens, Ph.D.*

In addition to our memories being altered by our current moods, circumstances, and misinformation, the *Journal of Neuroscience* reports that when we recall a memory, it is actually rare that we remember a complete and precise account of what happened; rather, we recall both accurate and erroneous information (even initially). Our memories are thus quite susceptible to distortion, and even dramatic distortion. Not only do we start with both accurate and erroneous information, but the memory becomes more and more subjected to gradual distortion every time it is recalled, and can even lead to mostly false recollection.[25]

During divorce, there are particular memories or stories that are recounted many, many times (both to oneself and to others). With each recollection, the memory gets altered and then resaved. Over time, we subconsciously change the details, change the nuances of those memories, and also change our relationship to the experiences themselves. This happens every time we retrieve a memory, and it can be influenced by external suggestions as well as our internal processing.

This is both disturbing and exciting. On one hand, it is unnerving because the more often you recall an event, the less you can rely on the accuracy of your memory.

On the other hand, you are now empowered with the awareness that your memories are malleable and, thus, you can decide to change your relationship to that memory. You can now be intentional about how you recall your memories: Do you want to recall them with hostility, or with curiosity? You can see how if you are thinking back on your memories of divorce with anger, it might get rewritten slightly differently than if you think back on them while feeling empathy or curiosity. In doing the latter, you can shift your heart-space toward one of healing and inner peace.

Changing Your Past

This empowerment is encouraging in the sense that even though we can't *undo* hurtful experiences of our past, we *can* change how we relate to them now.

You have control over how you experience your past.

Peace activist and Buddhist monk Thich Nhat Hanh explains:

The wrong thing done in the past is still there. And if you don't do anything, that wound—that pain—still continues. Suppose in the past you said something unkind to your mother. You really should not have said that thing to her, but you have done it… and your mother is no longer here for you to apologize to. Still, something is possible. With the purpose of deep looking, you recognize the wound and the suffering in yourself. Your mother is still in you, with the suffering. And you are also in there…in every cell in your body. So, with that kind of resentment, you breathe in and say "Sorry, Mommy. Sorry I have said that in the past to you. I am determined not to do it again. Please believe me. From now on, it will not happen again." Your "mother in you" will hear that right away and you will hear her smiling inside, in every cell of your body. And the wound begins to heal—very quickly—in the present moment.

They say that you cannot go back to the past and fix the past, but in this teaching and practice, you can. You can go back to the past and fix the wrong thing you have done in the past. Why? Because the wounds of the past are still there…disguised as the present moment. If you know how to touch the present moment deep enough, you touch the past. That is why you can mend the cut—you can heal the wound—right here and right now, because everything comes from the mind. The wrong mind has created the wound and now the right mind is healing the wound.[26]

Choosing your mindset, perspective, and emotional response toward your former spouse is important regardless of whether your lives stay intertwined or not. Even if you have the freedom to completely separate your lives after divorce, this practice is still useful because you will continue to have painful memories of your former partner, even though they are no longer directly involved in your life. Without doing this healing work, these memories will continue to cause you pain. It is for you to decide how you want to remember your relationship, your journey together, your divorce process, and your partner. Do you remember them with fondness and compassion? Do you appreciate what they brought into your life, despite having gone through struggles together? Or do you still harbor hurt and negative, caustic feelings?

You are in charge of how you recall your memories.

Just as you can shift the quality of your thoughts about your divorce and your former partner, you can also learn to relate to yourself with more feelings of compassion, humanity, appreciation, and recognition. When you think back on your relationship, your partner, and yourself, what do you notice? Do you feel overwhelmed? Broken? Disappointed in yourself? Frustrated? Victimized? All of those feelings elicit a certain response in the present moment. By shifting your relationship toward the events and people involved, you shift how your past is affecting you in the present and how you move forward from here.

What Else Is True?

If you're struggling to cultivate compassion and positive feelings toward your partner, remember that the first step in changing your feelings is changing your thoughts—the story you are telling yourself. Try broadening your perspective and stepping out of your tunnel view. Yes, there were probably instances of emotional distance or neglect during your marriage. Perhaps there was betrayal; perhaps there were greedy missteps your partner took, but undoubtedly there were positive, happy, loving moments as well.

When you are overwhelmed with hurt, fear, disappointment, and anger, it's easy to get fixated on the negative and stay trapped in this judgmental perspective. The labels you place on your former partner have subconsciously calcified into truths: You consider your former partner to be a "lazy slob," a "cheater," a "disengaged father," or an "overworking mother." In your tunnel view, these labels become definitive characteristics of your former partner. In order to soften your emotions and heal your wounds around the divorce, you will need to broaden your perspective, challenge those labels, and allow rays of sunlight to poke through the well-constructed walls of your dark tunnel.

Yes, you were frustrated by your partner. Yes, they behaved in hurtful ways. Still, ask yourself:

"What else is true?"

This does not negate the presence of those negative characteristics or behaviors. It does, however, balance them with a more objective, well-rounded view of the whole picture. It allows both sun and shadow to fill the space. It supports accuracy rather than simplistic categorization and labels. Both can be true and can coexist. Remember the concept of "both/and"? Ultimately, this more inclusive view opens the door and lets the light peek through, creating space for healing.

You Can't Control How They Respond

Cultivating a compassionate heart toward your former partner and maintaining loving boundaries for yourself are two of the fundamental principles that will provide stability for your ship as you navigate through divorce. You are tending to your internal well-being as well as promoting healthy dynamics with your partner. This will nourish your heart so that you may speak and act from the best of intentions.

That said, your partner's pain may obscure their vision. They may choose not to see or trust the state of your heart; they may accuse you of malintent or hidden motives; they may lash out at you in an effort to protect themselves.

Despite your best efforts and intentions, you cannot control how others think of you or respond to you.

You *can* control how you show up, but you *cannot* control how others see you. That is not yours to own. You cannot control their process, their responses, their perception of you, or their behavior. Release the tempting urge to try to control their perception of you. Do not alter your behavior in an attempt to make them see you differently. Rather, act in alignment with your highest self and do your best to cultivate a compassionate, peaceful heart while maintaining healthy boundaries and self-respect.

Let Go of Control

Another potential hinderance to your ability to let go, release, and move on with a peaceful heart is the driving urge to control what is happening, either by *insisting* that something happen or by *resisting* that something happen. Of course, you can influence its trajectory, but ultimately, what happens has a lot to do with the other person as well, and you are not in control of their decisions or behavior.

Maybe the decision at hand is whether to split up or stay together, or maybe it's a more subtle decision like how to move forward together as co-parents after divorce.

Which attitudes and mindsets do you want to cultivate? Grace, compassion, and understanding? Or bitterness, anger, and revenge?

Both of you are at full choice as to how you contribute to and influence this next iteration of your relationship. You can advocate for what you believe and stand assertively and compassionately in that place, yet regardless of how much you want something, it takes the other person to meet you there and be aligned in order for it to happen.

Therefore, do your best to express and assert what it is you need and want, and then recognize that the other person is also an independent being with free will. It is out of your control how your former partner responds to you—and to the divorce.

Also out of your control is how they talk about you and whether they cut you off from their friends and family. This can be deeply disturbing and sad, as you were once enmeshed with those people, their relationships, and their lives. Not only is this out of your control, but you often don't even *know* what they're saying. What tone are they using? What is the underlying message? Are they painting the whole picture?

If you have children together and you feel uncomfortable with them at your co-parent's house, it can be even scarier to think about what message the kids are being given. Coming to terms with the fact that you have little-to-no control over this can be gut-wrenching. If you are blessed to have a relatively conscious and committed co-parent, perhaps you are not so worried about the physical environment or discipline your children are exposed to, but you may still be worried about how your former partner talks to your kids about you. Are they letting their hurt and anger show through to the kids? Are they explicitly talking badly about you? Are they undermining you (whether intentional or not)? What subtleties are the kids going to pick up? How will this ultimately lead to shaping how they think and feel about you, and how they relate toward you?

These things are largely out of your control (unless, of course, the circumstances require court intervention). The more you can release your desperation to control it, the more you'll create space for your own healing.

---

*"Suffering persists when we hold tightly to that which
we cannot control." —Sharon Salzberg*

If someone is used to having influence over you and now no longer does, they can feel desperate to regain some of that control. Painting you as "the bad guy" can be an act of self-protection for your former partner because it then positions them as "the good guy." They become, in a sense, acquitted and are relieved of their need to take responsibility for their part in the breakup. By being the primary contact for that set of friends and family (or even the sole influencer of the kids when they're with them), they don't need to be worried about you overhearing or counteracting their stories; they might feel powerful and enjoy the feeling of self-justification that comes when they place the blame on you.

---

*In lieu of controlling you, they at least try to control
the image others have of you.*

The best way for you to combat these negative messages they might be putting out is to continue to cultivate *your* field of hope and healing; be aware of the picture you're painting about *them*; be objective when recounting the events of your story; take the high road and keep in mind that they, also, are a human being on a journey of learning and growth. You don't have to approve of their behavior, but you can hold underlying positive regard and compassion for them as a person while maintaining your boundaries and self-respect. Your positivity and goodwill will come back to you tenfold and will be visible to those around you. This attitude paints a stronger picture than anything your former spouse can say negatively about you.

Who they say you are is not necessarily the truth of who you are.

Their process is their process; their journey is their journey; the story they tell themselves and others is their story. The choice of whether to throw fertilizer or herbicide on the joint field of your current relationship is up to them. You are not in control of it and must release the desire to control it in order to promote your own inner healing.

Stand confidently, knowing who you are at your core. Continue to be openhearted and speak generously, albeit accurately, about and toward your partner. Try to maintain civility and respect wherever possible. Yes, there will probably be some bridges burned and some people who no longer want to interact with you because they have chosen sides and want to keep their alliances pure. That's the nature of divorce. Still, you can hold your head high, knowing that you've done everything you can to maintain openheartedness and warmth despite the picture being painted of you. Those things are out of your control, and the sooner you can learn to release them, the sooner you can cultivate that sense of inner peace.

Let Go of the Positive Things As Well

Not only do you need to practice letting go of *negative things* that are beyond your control, but also letting go of *positive things* that are slipping away and are beyond your control.

- Perhaps you hate the idea of sharing your children with your former spouse and are trying desperately to show evidence that sabotages their chance of being awarded partial custody; you don't want to let go of your kids.

- Perhaps your relationship with your children has become strained and you're trying everything you can think of to make them like you again; you don't want to let go of that close connection you once felt with them.

- Perhaps you're grieving the fact that you need to move out of your home that you've been building and nesting in for years; you don't want to let go of that home—that time shared and those memories made.

Whatever it is, this desperation to hold onto things you cherish also can create great stress and angst.

Absolutely—do what you can to influence those things and keep your determination sacred. Don't let apathy set in when you feel like all hope is lost. At the same time, know that despite your best efforts, some things might slip away from your grasp. Again, the principle is applicable:

Do your best and let go of the rest.

Doing the inner work of cultivating a peaceful heart during divorce does not keep you from struggle and it does not anesthetize you from pain and anger. Rather, it gives you the tools to recover from those events more quickly: The pain incurred will be less destructive and less caustic to your soul. You will be able to move forward in life with more ease, grace, love, and well-being.

Practices to Help You Let Go

When we desperately seek the permanence of good relationships and experiences, we create undue stress for ourselves. Likewise, when we feel a desperate desire to keep bad experiences away, we also create stress (due to the intensity of the aversion or repulsion). Seeing as intense attraction and aversion both create stress when we try to control them, we would do well to let go of our need to control these things. In so doing, we can more easily accept life's undulations, maintaining a sense of inner peace and calm despite the ups and downs.

Here are four short practices you can adopt that will help train your brain and heart to release control of the things you cannot change.

Prayer

The Serenity Prayer by Reinhold Niebuhr is a short yet profound prayer that can easily be framed or placed in a visible location—a simple reminder and salve for the disconcerted soul:

*"God, grant me the serenity to accept the things
I cannot change, courage to change the things I can,
and wisdom to know the difference."*

Mindful Breathing Mantra

We return to our previously mentioned one-breath mindfulness and self-compassion practice, as it is quite powerful. It can be used throughout your day and is especially helpful during moments of exasperation and overwhelm.

Breathe deeply in and out one time while repeating this mantra to yourself and letting your body sink into the knowledge of it:

"I breathe in, I do my best.
I breathe out, I let go of the rest."

Meditation: Let Your Emotions Come and Go Like Clouds in the Sky

This dedicated meditation practice trains your mind to let both good and bad experiences in life come and go with ease. It helps you release the need for the permanence of good things and the elimination of the bad through the acknowledgement of the transient nature of all experiences.

Close your eyes or soften them while you read. Take a few moments to settle your mind, letting your thoughts settle down slowly, like the snow in a snow globe.

Notice your breathing, your inbreath and your outbreath. As you breathe deeply, notice the rise and fall of your chest. Notice the expansion and contraction of your rib cage.

As you breathe out, let your body relax…getting more and more relaxed with each outbreath.

Let your body become heavy, melting into the surface that's supporting you.

Imagine yourself lying on a blanket in a field of grass, looking up at the beautiful sky. Let yourself sink into that blanket, totally at peace, feeling the sunlight on your skin.

Notice the color of the sky. Notice what's on the horizon. Notice any clouds that might be in your sky.

As you lie there looking up at the sky, notice how the clouds move.

Notice how they shift. Notice how they change shape.

Sometimes they become thinner, wispy clouds that eventually dissolve and reveal pure blue sky.

Sometimes they become bigger, joining together in size and density.

Notice these building clouds grow, getting darker and heavier... now forming menacing thunderclouds. As the whole sky darkens, the storm builds...the air is thick with the scent of incoming rain.

These storm clouds reach capacity and soon begin their torrential downpour, sending lightning and thunder into the sky.

You witness the fury and the magnificence of the storm, in all its power.

Eventually, the storm begins to die down. The rain stops.

The clouds begin to clear, and sunlight pokes its rays through the holes.

Gradually, the clouds thin, becoming more and more sparse.

You find yourself lying once again under a beautifully sunny sky.

Take a few moments to breathe, noticing what it was like to witness the sky as the storm passed through.

The sky is your landscape. It is your being, your existence, your life.

The clouds are the experiences and emotions that come and go throughout your minutes, days, weeks, and years.

Sometimes life is a sunny day—nourishing, warm, and pleasant. Other times, monsoon storms rage for days on end.

These feelings and experiences are temporary. They are transient, shifting in every moment. Always changing shape—gathering, thundering, calming, and dispersing.

So are your emotions and experiences in life: ever changing, ever shifting. Sunny days will not last forever, nor will the intense thunderstorms persist.

Storms will come. Let them. Do not resist them. Be with them. Learn from them. And let them pass when they are ready. They will move on. You will have sunny days again.

Take a few moments to breathe, feeling your body, feeling your breath.

Wiggle your fingers. Wiggle your toes. Gently open your eyes, stretch, and come back to the present moment.

Remember how it felt to be watching the ever-changing sky. Whenever you are overcome with all-consuming emotions or experiences, liken them to a weather system rolling into your existence. This weather system—this experience—might unleash its fury, but it is ever changing, ever shifting. It will dissipate. It will move on.

Metaphors

By being in a state of peace and acceptance about the natural flow and rhythm of life and by allowing it to take its course, you invite room for more ease and spaciousness as you go through your experiences. If you remain adamant and rigid in trying to control the events of life, you will likely experience more friction and resistance as you go along. The more you can allow for the ebb and flow of life, the more peaceful you can be.

In a battle between the rock and the water,
the water always wins.

This is not to say that you need to be resigned to things happening without taking action to create the life you want. On the contrary, water is powerful and can carve its own path—it is a force to be reckoned with. As with water, be proactive about creating the life you want—set your sights on what you want and work for those dreams. As you do this, allow for flow, let go of control, and recognize that there will be bumps and obstacles along the way that you cannot control. Remember, struggle is optional.

Rest in self-confidence, knowing that you can get through these moments in one way or another. Learning how to shift and flow with these natural undulations in life can help you to become adaptable and resilient. It's like learning how to become a supple reed in the wind: If you are strict and rigid, holding firmly to the need for things to go a certain way, you will snap in half when the wind blows too hard in a certain direction.

Learn to bend in the wind, not fight against it.
Remain strong, tall, and supple,
with your roots holding firm.

As with the metaphors of the water and the reeds, so it is with divorce.

Learn to do your best in each moment and then let go of the need for it to look a certain way. Know that you can adapt and shift to the new normal—and that this new normal will also be temporary. Things are naturally in a constant state of flux, movement, and change. Nothing is forever.

Knowing what to predict can alleviate fear and stress; yet, during divorce, there is so much unknown. If there is one thing we can be certain of in divorce, it is that there *will be uncertainty and stress* during this journey. If we go into it eyes wide open, knowing that we are entering into uncharted territory (which brings a certain amount of innate fear and risk), we can accept the presence of these unsettling feelings with less resistance. It's less scary because we expect its presence.

"Courage is a love affair with the unknown."
—Osho

Cor (or *heart* in Latin) is the root of "courage." Courage stems from your heart. Set your intentions toward cultivating a peaceful heart, while still having strong boundaries. Connect to this purest version of your heart, following it as you navigate through the unknown, and you will build a sense of inner resonance and trust that will lead you through to the other side.

This is a time of change, of transition, of breaking down, and of rebirth. You are resilient. You will feel lost along the way. You will likely incur wounds. And you will come out of it having gained knowledge, compassion, life experience, and understanding. You will be a new person.

Kintsugi—Honor Your Journey

In Japanese culture, there is a beautiful art form called *kintsugi*.

When a piece of pottery becomes cracked or broken, it is not necessarily thrown away just because it is broken—its broken state is not something to be ashamed of and despised. Instead, a *kintsugi* artist might carefully reassemble the broken pieces, filling the cracks with a special lacquer infused with silver or gold, which highlights the repaired seams. The artist is calling attention to this part of the object's journey, honoring its process of brokenness and restoration. The object is now looked upon with reverence and has even become more valuable; it has experienced the ups and downs of life, and it has endured.

What if we responded to divorce in a similar way? What if this part of our life is embraced and even highlighted with gold because it is such a rich part in making us who we are today? We have, after all, been through struggle and pain and come out of it with newly acquired knowledge, resilience, and strength. We have experienced transformation and rebirth. What if, instead of being ashamed of your journey of divorce, you recognize that it, too, is a part of your human journey?

You can choose how this journey affects you. It may not shift overnight, but it will shift with conscious intention.

PRINCIPLE 5

CHOOSE YOUR CREW WISELY

 CAPTAIN'S LOG

"For my own liberation, I aim to stand tall and confidently in who I am, nurturing compassion toward my former partner—doing my best to promote healing between us while maintaining healthy boundaries for myself. I consciously choose to surround myself with people that instinctually support these goals instead of people who rile me up more, widening the divide I feel with my former partner. My entourage can be tremendously influential in shaping how I process my emotions and how I experience divorce. I owe it to myself to be selective about who I share my inner journey with, choosing only those people who will naturally point me toward my goals of healthy perspectives and healing.

By allowing my trusted crew to witness my journey, I give myself the gift of belonging, support, and affirmation. This crew will help me stay connected to my deep inner knowledge that I am worthy of love and a capable captain of my ship." —S.M.

Be Intentional About Whom You Choose

Your crew members are the people who will journey beside you, helping you navigate your ship through the storm. Be intentional about whom you bring aboard your ship, looking for those who will keep you stable, with your hull weighted, as opposed to those who seem to be "good friends," siding with you no matter what. These "good friends" provide a false sense of stability but will ultimately end up contributing to—and exacerbating—your imbalance.

Early on in my divorce, I remember talking with several people who had gone through their own experience of divorce. Many were still deeply afflicted with rancor toward their ex-partners. It was tempting to be drawn into their stories and, likewise, to draw them into mine—uniting as allies against our common enemy: our exes.

Yet, here I was, attempting to consciously cultivate a peaceful heart. As I engaged in these conversations, I realized: I didn't *want* to surround myself with people who were going to augment the frustration, rage, and indignation I was already feeling. I didn't *want* to be around someone who encouraged me to sit in the muck and feel victimized as we wallowed together. I didn't *want* to be around people who furthered the divide that was already between us. The rift was already there. It was deep, strong, and full of emotion, as at that point, we were right in the thick of it. I didn't want to make it worse.

Instead, I wanted to be with people who would help me heal. People who would help *us* heal—as co-parents and ex-partners. I wanted to be with people who would help me calibrate toward fairness and equitability, not conspirators who would support my position without first discerning whether my stance seemed reasonable.

Be Wary of Supporters Who Add Timber to Your Fire

Be on the lookout for these so-called good friends: those who affirm and bolster who you are and what you are feeling, those who get riled up out of indignation at how you are being treated, and those who occasionally berate and belittle your former partner out of solidarity and well-intentioned protection of you.

These supporters add fuel to your fire, making your flame of fury burn even brighter than it already was. This inevitably makes you feel emboldened, righteous, and justified in the moment (which feels really good!), but will ultimately create a larger divide between you and your former partner by encouraging you to dig in your heels, harden your heart, and become entrenched in your stance.

As tempting as it may seem to gather a team of people who commiserate with you and embolden your indignation, this is neither healthy nor supportive of your process. Though they are genuine and well intentioned in their support, their influence can be insidious. It becomes almost intoxicating to be around them because they reinforce the idea that you are reasonable and justified—contrary to your partner, who is being outrageous and is fully to blame! Be wary of:

- People who deepen the divide between you and your former partner.

- People who affirm your victimhood and thereby enable the pain.

- People who are going to reinforce a decidedly negative view of your former partner.

- People who blindly support you without encouraging self-reflection and self-critique (coupled with self-compassion).

Be extremely conscientious about whom you choose to surround yourself with and whom you are willing to accept into your life at this point. Be vigilant about letting even the smallest breach puncture this conscious environment you are working so hard to create for yourself. Even if it seems innocuous to rail against your former partner in the privacy of your own home with a good friend and a bottle of wine, it is not healthy. It reinforces the victimhood and judgmental sentiments you are trying to overcome, and it releases negative energy into the world.

The intentional work you are doing to cultivate a peaceful heart is, in fact, your armor against perpetuating the rage and hostility. This shifted framework of thinking is nascent and, as such, may still be quite fragile and susceptible to influence. But it is a precious and valuable asset, worth protecting fiercely. It will serve you best to recognize these well-intentioned yet counterproductive supporters who add fuel to your fire—and not invite them in at all. Preserve the sanctuary you are creating for your heart; be selective about whom you let in.

Choose Those Who Will Sit by the Fire with You

A healthier choice is to surround yourself with people who will absolutely support you, and, at the same time, help you stay calibrated, reasonable, and thoughtful.

This type of supporter is one who listens to your feelings with compassion and then conveys their confidence that you will respond well to that situation, someone who can be with your fire while it burns yet does not add more fuel. This supporter sits with you in your intense emotion, yet they also encourage you to step outside your anger and explore a different perspective for a moment. They may play the devil's advocate or help you connect back to your guiding principles of self-respect and compassion. They can be with your intense emotions but will also help you return to a calm, grounded, reasonable stance.

These supporters promote healthy self-advocacy and healing.

Choose Those Who Can Wholeheartedly Support You...and Your Former Spouse

When you are in the thick of emotions, it's hard to remove yourself enough to get perspective about what is realistic or reasonable, and what is not. Your intentionally selected crew can help you get there. Specifically:

- Choose people who can help calibrate both your expectations and your view of reality. They will earnestly help you identify reasonable middle ground as you navigate through conflict. They will hear your story and see your heart but are not going to allow you to bathe in victimhood.

- Choose people who can see the humanity in both you and your former partner—who understand that you are two good people, going through hurtful, painful, sad times; that you are two good people who are struggling; that you both have good hearts, despite destructive choices you may have made; that you are both people who were doing your best in the given circumstances; that despite your struggles, choices, and behaviors, you both are still worthy, respectable, loving people at your core.[*]

- Choose people who will ultimately help you bridge the divide you are feeling with your former partner. They will promote healthy relationships, not discord and contentiousness.

---

[*]A small minority of people may not, in fact, still be good people. For the most part though, this sentiment is applicable.

♦ Choose people who genuinely want the best for not only you, but also your former partner—people who continue to support you both as parents and as people; who want wellness and prosperity for you both; and who want to support you both in your respective life journeys, even though your marriage has ended.

These are the people who can rise above the contentiousness of the moment and help you move forward toward healing. They are love amplifiers and grace generators.

Hiding Struggles Perpetuates Shame

Having a handpicked crew to journey beside you through this storm is paramount. Trying to navigate it by yourself means paving the way for more intensity, fear, pain, and isolation.

Let your crew see your struggles and accompany you through this journey. If you are hiding your feelings in the dark, inaccessible corners of your soul, it is often because you fear you will be judged for them. You then put up a façade, hide your truth, and mask your struggle in an effort to be loved and accepted. This erodes your sense of self and creates a false belief that you must be different from who you are in order to be loved.

When you feel ashamed of your authentic self, you want to hide even more. Then you begin to doubt that you are truly a good person, worthy of love and belonging just as you are—as a human, struggling through the ups and downs of life.

The fact is, we all struggle. We all have felt embarrassed or ashamed at times. We all know what it's like to feel "less than." The more you can embrace your authentic self and let this imperfect self be seen, the more self-confident you will become. You are giving yourself the opportunity to be authentically loved and supported for who you are, not for who you portray yourself to be.

Vulnerability Creates Connection

Not only does this vulnerability lead to increased self-confidence, it also leads to connection.

By confiding in someone, they receive confirmation that they are part of your in-group. As we have seen, this increases their capacity to connect empathetically with you. They feel your pain, they can relate to your pain, and they often self-identify with similar pain they've experienced over the course of their lives. This gives you the commonality of shared experience: Even if it wasn't the same circumstance, you share the same feeling, and that creates a bond between you.

Be courageous and let your close companions see your hurt, your sorrows, and your confusion. Let them into your world so they can be a sounding board and a place of solace. They likely have wisdom to share, perspectives that may help, and boundless love that will replenish your tank.

By letting your underbelly show, you create the opportunity for connection and you offer your supporter a precious gift as well.

Vulnerability Is a Gift to the Other Person

Think about it: When a friend is struggling and turns to you for a listening ear, a shoulder to cry on, or some much-needed support and advice, doesn't it feel great? Of course it does! It's a wonderful feeling to be needed, to be of service to someone, and to feel trustworthy and useful. You are making a difference.

Sharing your vulnerability with another tells them: "I trust you. You are valuable. I am glad you are here and I appreciate you. Thank you for being here and for supporting me." Simply by sharing your struggle, you offer them affirmation that they matter—that they have a valuable impact in the world, just by being who they are.

When you isolate in shame, you not only perpetuate that shame, but also deprive the other person of the opportunity to be of service—to be needed. It is a *gift* to them when you reach out and let them into your world.

Sadly, we can be so hesitant to reach out when we need help or support. It can make a person feel scared, raw, and emotionally naked. Yet, more often than not, we find camaraderie and shared experience when we let our guard down and let another person into our world.

In isolation, we assume we are in it alone.
In connection, we find support, commonality,
and companionship.

Being strong does not mean always being composed and knowing what you want. Sometimes being strong means having the self-confidence to admit that you are broken and confused. Sometimes being strong means asking others for advice, support, and direction. Sometimes being strong means admitting you've made mistakes. Sometimes being strong means asking for forgiveness. Sometimes being strong means asking for a hug and seeking wisdom from others.

Letting people in when you feel broken can feel scary. Asking for help can seem like you are admitting weakness and inadequacy. Confessing that you are aching and weary can feel like conceding defeat. It feels safer and much more comfortable to hide behind a well-constructed façade, shielding your ego and your fragile sense of identity. Yet, in actuality, it makes your sense of self more tenuous and susceptible to wounding.

Vulnerability Is Also a Gift to You

If you do not let people in—if you put on armor and protect the vulnerable parts of you from being seen—you are, in essence, portraying only the shiny, well-put-together sides of yourself. Of course people will know and love the shiny self you are showing them. But it undermines your healing because the raw, hurting parts of you remain unseen by others and this perpetuates your shame and insecurities.

This desire to hide your insecurities and missteps is subtle; it happens so gradually that you don't always notice you're doing it. But as you hide more and more of your journey from others, it becomes more difficult to let yourself be seen, valued, and respected as a whole person. It becomes threatening to let them see the more broken sides of you because you don't want them to lose respect for you.

Yes, there is a risk that you will share "too much" and that some people will turn away from you when they learn about struggles you are having or decisions you have made—that *is* a real possibility. Perhaps they don't approve of you or perhaps they don't want to deal with that in their lives. Though it might hurt to lose that person from your life, there is also a gift in it: The people who are left are your authentic supporters. These are the ones who love you for who you are, in good times and in bad, the ones who will stay by your side as you journey through life. They are your authentic friends, supporters, and companions. Don't hide yourself in fear that others will abandon you; let that selection process happen naturally and appreciate the gift in it. Then let your whole self heal and blossom.

If people love *the whole you* during the most difficult moments of your life, you can be assured that they will love you in the other moments as well. In fact, these people will probably look upon you with admiration, seeing you as a person of strength, confident enough in your intrinsic worth that you aren't afraid to let others see your messiness. You are likely becoming a source of inspiration for them, showing them that they also have permission to seek help when they need it. You're showing them that they don't need to be embarrassed or ashamed about their struggles. You never know what gift you're giving others just by the example you set when you allow yourself to be seen and you invite others into your journey.

"Don't be afraid to share your story. It might be the key to someone else's prison." —TobyMac

---

By letting your supporters witness your turbulent journey of emotions, they are given the privilege of seeing all sides of you; they are being given implicit permission to show more sides of themselves, and you are building your self-confidence by truly being seen and known during some of your lowest times. You are giving yourself the gift of being known and loved for who you intrinsically are—a strong, capable person who has been rocked by emotion and trials yet is still worthy of love.

If you selectively let yourself be known and affirmed only during the good times, it sets you up for feeling a sense of conditional love. You lose out on the richness of knowing that you are loved—and *loveable*—even during the dark times.

How affirming it is when you can be a full person— shadows and all—and still be loved!

By showing your underbelly to your supporters, you begin to experience unconditional love.

Again, it all comes from choosing your crew: Who is it that you want on your ship? What type of environment do you want to create for yourself now and moving forward? What type of attitude do you want to have when approaching or thinking about your former partner? Choose people to surround yourself with that promote the qualities you care about having as you move forward. Then, let these people into your inner world; let them understand the raw landscape of your emotions and your current experiences; let them know your struggles and your fears.

Having these supporters can help you maintain a hold on reality and help you stay connected to who you are at your core, despite the barrage of attacks that are coming your way (whether from your former spouse, from your own self-beratement, or from others). These supporters are invaluable mirrors, reflecting back what you cannot see for yourself. They help you maintain a backbone when you feel weak. They help calibrate you when you are enraged.

You have the opportunity to robustly grow your self-confidence by letting a select group of people see the whole you and witness all of your journey, by letting them know you and love you for who you are in the moment, even in the midst of a seemingly relentless, stormy experience.

By surrounding yourself with these crew members, you will feel that—regardless of your storm, your fluctuating emotions, and your struggle—you are *known*, you are *enough*, you are *worthy*, you are *loved*, and you are *respected*. All of these messages may be in direct opposition to the messages of your former partner. What a treasure to have authentic, enthusiastic supporters; what a valuable resource in times of self-doubt and obscured vision. By being known fully in your darkest hour and still respected and loved, you will increase your resilience, strength, and self-confidence.

ONWARD

 CAPTAIN'S LOG

"I am navigating through a tempestuous storm. On every tack and with every interaction, I am choosing to keep my sights focused on my North Star: Compassion. I am cultivating an open heart, accompanied by loving boundaries and self-respect. I will surround myself with a crew who will support me in this. I may be struggling and feel off course, yet I need not be ashamed of who I am or where I am in life. Storms happen; I will persevere. My journey is my own. I am compassionate toward myself and my former partner and I am focused on healing. How I navigate through this tempest will affect how I look back upon this time. I can choose to imbue my journey with bitterness, remorse, sorrow, and anger—fighting against the forces; or I can choose to move through it with compassion, growth, worthiness, and strength. With my handpicked crew and my reinforced ballast, my ship will remain upright and structurally sound as I sail North toward calmer weather. My peaceful heart will prevail." —S.M.

Go forth on your journey in life. There will be raging tempests and pounding storms. There will be beautiful, calm days of sailing and peaceful, star-filled nights. Such is the journey of life, and this journey is yours to be lived.

As you navigate through this time,

May your hull be stable,
May your heart be at peace,
And may you remain ever-pointed
toward the North Star of Compassion.

EPILOGUE

If there is light in the soul,
There will be beauty in the person.

If there is beauty in the person,
There will be harmony in the home.

If there is harmony in the home,
There will be order in the nation.

If there is order in the nation,
There will be peace in our world.

—Chinese Proverb

ADDITIONAL RESOURCES

Though you may be tempted to view divorce as a time of breaking down, of the dissolution of dreams, and of the crumbling of your identity, I invite you to broaden your view and consider that this might, in fact, be a period of rebirth for you. What is opening up for you that otherwise would not have been possible?

Perhaps there is a beautiful metamorphosis taking place. Sometimes "what is" needs to get demolished in order to create "what will be." Just because it is painful does not mean it is unhealthy or unnecessary; just because you are aching, it does not mean that beauty cannot emerge from the rubble. Not all pain leads to further injury. Sometimes, pain leads to growth.

Oftentimes, the most painful experiences in life are also the ones that create newness, growth, and the blossoming of something that otherwise could not have been. Pain accompanies transformation.

Consider childbirth: This process of transition is called labor for a reason—it is a lot of work and involves a lot of pain. It is accompanied by stress, tension, tears, and overwhelm. But it is in service of *birthing a new life*—of ushering someone through this tight space, transitioning them from the womb to the outside world. It is tight and probably unpleasant and painful for the baby as he squeezes through the birth canal, but this tight squeeze actually helps him afterward. The constriction around his chest as he travels through the canal helps expel the fluid from his lungs so he can effectively breathe when he is born. Babies born through C-section have four times as many admissions to the ICU due to respiratory problems; the tight squeeze is actually healthy for the baby, constricting as it may be. [27]

So it is with divorce. While in the midst of it, it can be hard to consider that the pain might be in service of your growth, or that this transition could open the door for something even more beautiful (albeit different from what you had imagined).

You don't yet know who you will be when you emerge, but you do know you are growing, changing, and will emerge a different person. Cultivate your field, cultivate your heart. It will affect who you are as you blossom into the next phase of your life. Look for the blessings in the shift and anticipate the strength and wisdom that you will acquire by going through it.

At some point, you will feel your world starting to equalize; your sense of stasis will start to return.

The question then becomes: What's next for me? What am I learning from this? What's good about having had this experience? What would need to happen in order for me to look back on this as one of the most positive turning points in my life? What is possible from here?

"You are pure potential."
—Martin de Maat

This is a time to get more clarity about who you are in this new phase of life. Where are you now? What are your values? What do you stand for? What do you believe in? What stirs your passion in life? What is it that you, as a unique individual, bring to this world?

To paraphrase the author and theologian Frederick Buechner:

Your purpose is where your deep passion meets the world's great hunger.

Connecting to your purpose can help give you something to focus on during this transition, and also help you blossom post-divorce. In this stage of recovery and growth, stay open to new possibilities that you might otherwise not have imagined. You are likely quite a different person than you were before your divorce.

Finding answers for these types of questions is easier said than done, particularly when you're in the midst of such upheaval. Friends and loved ones can certainly help you find clarity. Additionally, there are trained professionals—life coaches—who can help you fast-track this process. A life coach is someone who partners with you in a creative process to help you become the best version of yourself. They help you look at where you are today and where you want to be in the future, and then help you take precise action to get there. They listen deeply and trust that you have the answers you seek. They are trained in asking powerful questions that help you discover your truth.

Many people have heard of coaching but are not really sure what it is. Some associate it with therapy, but they are actually quite different (and complementary) approaches. To understand more of the subtleties:

- A therapist typically helps you go from struggling to neutral, whereas a life coach helps you go from neutral to thriving.

- A therapist helps you heal from your past, whereas a life coach helps you envision and create your future.

- A therapist is someone whom we typically look to for answers, whereas a coach helps us look within for our own answers.

- Just as a physical therapist is there to help athletes recover from physical injury, a therapist helps us recover from emotional injury. Likewise, just as a sports coach helps athletes optimize their form, tactics, and performance, a life coach helps you optimize your habits, thoughts, and actions so that you can live your best life with success, purpose, and healthy relationships.

Whether you reach out to a professional or a friend, I encourage you to bring someone in on this journey of exploration. It's more fun and often much more revealing than doing it yourself! Seek someone with a listening ear and an open heart; someone who can help you search for your truth, support you in staying aligned with your North Star, and encourage you onward toward the manifestation of your life purpose.

For some, this shift from surviving to thriving will happen sooner than later. For others, it may be more gradual. It may take time to find your new normal and rebuild life from the ashes of divorce. Whatever your rhythm, whatever your process, be gentle with yourself and stay connected to your inner light. You will emerge as a person with more life experience, wisdom, and perspective.

May you go forth with blessings, healing, and renewed confidence as you journey forth into this next phase of life. With steadfast intention and steady progress, you *can* and *will* achieve a more peaceful heart as you navigate divorce. In fact, you are already on your way.

Journey well, courageous soul.

May you be well,
may you be loved,
and may your heart be at peace.

ABOUT THE AUTHOR

Stephanie Meriaux is an avid mindfulness practitioner, certified coach, and the founder of the Relationship Bootcamp.

She has worked as a project manager for GIS companies in both the United States and France and holds a B.S. in mathematics. She also earned her Associate Certified Coach (ACC) certification through the International Coach Federation (ICF) and her Certified Professional Co-Active Coach (CPCC) certification from the Co-Active Training Institute (CTI)—the "gold standard" of coaching schools—and is a graduate of CTI's intensive Co-Active Leadership Program.

Stephanie is additionally a certified Search Inside Yourself (SIY) teacher. Search Inside Yourself is a world-renowned training program born at Google and based on neuroscience. It teaches practical mindfulness, emotional intelligence, and leadership tools to help you unlock your full potential at work and in life. Its elite group of teachers has brought SIY to over 50 countries and served more than 50,000 people, including all civil government staff and teachers in the nation of Bhutan.

She founded the Relationship Bootcamp, a four-month intensive designed to help couples find more love, joy, and connection without going to therapy, and has written this book for couples who are already past that point, and are aching for healing, hope, and inner calm.

176

You can find the Relationship Bootcamp at
www.RelationshipBootcamp.us

Stephanie is available for speaking engagements, individual
and relationship coaching, workshop and retreat facilitation, and
corporate mindfulness and emotional intelligence trainings. She
can be reached at

www.StephanieMeriaux.com

**Working together, we can raise humanity's baseline of
connection, happiness, and purpose.**

Illuminate your essence—
Shine from within and light up the world.

WORKS CITED

1 Jacob Feldman. 2016. "The Simplicity Principle in Perception and Cognition." *WIREs Cognitive Science* 7:330–340. doi: 10.1002/wcs.1406.

2 Wikipedia. 2020. "Gaslighting." https://en.wikipedia.org/wiki/ Gaslighting.

3 Michael Fulwiler. 2015. "#AskGottman: Affairs." The Gottman Institute. https://www.gottman.com/blog/askgottman-affairs/.

4 Ryan Holiday. 2016. *The Daily Stoic: 366 Meditations on Wisdom, Perseverance, and the Art of Living.* New York: Portfolio/ Penguin.

5 Sharon Salzberg. 1999. *A Heart as Wide as the World: Stories on the Path of Lovingkindness.* Boulder, Colorado: Shambhala.

6 Wikipedia. 2020. "Amygdala Hijack." https://en.wikipedia.org/ wiki/Amygdala_hijack.

7 Jean Decety and Claus Lamm. 2006. "Human Empathy through the Lens of Social Neuroscience." *Scientific World Journal* 6:1146–1163. doi: 10.1100/tsw.2006.221.

8 David Eagleman. 2015. "Episode 5: In-Group/
Out-Group." PBS. https://www.pbs.org/video/
brain-david-eagleman-episode-5-in-group-out-group/.

9 Andrea Serino, Giulia Giovagnoli, and Elisabetta Ladavas.
2009. "I Feel What You Feel If You Are Similar To Me." PLoS
One 4(3):e4930. doi: 10.1371/journal.pone.0004930.

10 Grit Hein, Giorgia Silani, Kerstin Preuschoff, Daniel Batson,
and Tania Singer. 2010. "Neural Responses to Ingroup and
Outgroup Members' Suffering Predict Individual Differences
in Costly Helping." *Neuron* 68:149–160. doi: 10.1016/j.
neuron.2010.09.003.

11 Tania Singer, Ben Seymour, John P. O'Doherty, Klaas
E. Stephan, Raymond J. Dolan, and Chris D. Frith. 2006.
"Empathic Neural Responses Are Modulated by the Perceived
Fairness of Others." *Nature* 439(7075):466–469. doi: 10.1038/
nature04271.

12 Bruce Lipton. 2014. *The Honeymoon Effect: The Science of
Creating Heaven on Earth.* Carlsbad, CA: Hay House Inc.

13 Caroline Williams. 2017. "Different Meditation Types
Train Distinct Parts of Your Brain." NewScientist. https://www.
newscientist.com/article/2149489-different-meditation-types-
train-distinct-parts-of-your-brain/.

14 Harvard. 2011. "In the Journals: Mindfulness Meditation
Practice Changes the Brain." Harvard Women's Health
Watch. https://www.health.harvard.edu/mind-and-mood/
mindfulness-meditation-practice-changes-the-brain.

15 Ibid.

16 National Domestic Violence Hotline. "Why Do People Abuse?" Accessed Aug 7, 2020. https://www.thehotline.org/is-this-abuse/why-do-people-abuse/.

17 The Gottman Institute. 2020. "Research FAQ." https://www.gottman.com/about/research/faq/.

18 The Gottman Institute. 2020. "Research." https://www.gottman.com/about/research/.

19 Maria Cohut. 2019 "Can Scientists 'Hack' Memory?" Medical News Today. https://www.medicalnewstoday.com/articles/324900#Memory-recall-and-forgetting.

20 William Shiel. 2017. "Medical Definition of Neuroplasticity." MedicineNet. https://www.medicinenet.com/script/main/art.asp?articlekey=40362.

21 Marla Paul. 2012. "Your Memory Is Like the Telephone Game." Northwestern Now. https://news.northwestern.edu/stories/2012/09/your-memory-is-like-the-telephone-game.

22 Anne Trafton. 2017. "How We Recall the Past." MIT News. http://news.mit.edu/2017/neuroscientists-discover-brain-circuit-retrieving-memories-0817.

23 Kendra Cherry. 2020. "The Misinformation Effect and False Memories." VeryWellMind. https://www.verywellmind.com/what-is-the-misinformation-effect-2795353.

24 Ibid.

25 Donna Bridge and Ken Paller. 2012. "Neural Correlates of Reactivation and Retrieval-Induced Distortion." *Journal of Neuroscience* 32(35):12144–12151. doi: 10.1523 JNEUROSCI.1378-12.2012.

26 Thich Nhat Hanh. June 20, 2004. "How Do We Deal With Regrets?" Speech. Plum Village, France.

27 British Medical Journal. 2020. "Elective Caesareans Carry Increased Risk Of Breathing Problems." ScienceDaily. www.sciencedaily.com/releases/2007/12/071212202023.htm.

INDEX

meditation exercises
    4-5-6 Breathing, 71–72
    Breathing Meditation, 72–74
    Guided Weather Visualization,
      143–145
    Just Like Me and
      Lovingkindness, 91–93
    Self-Compassion Breathing
      Mantra, 71, 143
    See also attention, awareness,
      brain training
memories, 130–135
mental framework, 11–17, 86, 155
metaphors, 146–147
mindfulness, 87–88, 143
mindset, 81, 130, 134, 138
mirror neurons, 82, 83, 91–93
misinformation effect, 131–132

N
negative sentiment override, 34–35,
    38, 85
neocortex, 69–70
neurons, 82, 83, 89, 131
neuroplasticity, 89, 131
    See also change
non-duality, 8, 14–16
    See also both/and view, either/
      or view
North Star, 59, 61, 63, 75, 165, 167,
    174

O
objectivity, 37, 38, 47, 140, 148
    See also observing eye
observing eye, 36–40, 49, 117–118
openheartedness, 94, 140
    See also compassion
out-group, 83, 86

P
paradigm. *See* mental framework
parasympathetic nervous system, 70
parenting, 44, 48–50, 111, 119,
    138–139
passivity, 108, 109
peace
    by appeasement, 22, 103,
      108–110
    definition of, 11, 53
    despite anger, 52
    through changing memories,
      130–134
    through compassion, 63–67,
      74–75, 141
    through curiosity, 23
    through letting go of control,
      137–148
    through non-judgment, 37,
      40, 43
    through owning your part,
      45–46
    through shifted mindset,
      11–13
    See also brain training, healing
perceiving eye, 36–40, 49, 51,
    117–118
perpetrators, 21–23
personal identity, 1, 65–67, 122, 159
prayer, 142

R
relationship
    as its own entity, 121–122
    establishing new norms,
      103–115
    progression of deterioration,
      84–86
    tending the field, 127, 140
rest-and-digest response, 70
revenge, 83, 86, 90, 103

CPSIA information can be obtained
at www.ICGtesting.com
Printed in the USA
LVHW080323171020
668893LV00006B/763